Military Acquisition Costs

The Effects of Lean Manufacturing

Cynthia R. Cook • John C. Graser

Prepared for the United States Air Force

Approved for public release; distribution unlimited

Project AIR FORCE **RAND**

The research reported here was sponsored by the United States Air Force under Contract F49842-96-C-0001. Further information may be obtained from the Strategic Planning Division, Directorate of Plans, Hq USAF.

Library of Congress Cataloging-in-Publication Data

Cook, Cynthia R., 1965-
  Military airframe acquisition costs : the effects of lean manufacturing /
Cynthia R. Cook, John C. Graser.
    p. cm.
  "MR-1325."
  Includes bibliographical references.
  ISBN 0-8330-3023-X
  1. Airplanes, Military—Design and construction—Costs. 2. Airplanes,
Military—Design and construction—Quality control. 3. Aerospace industries—
Cost control. I. Graser, John C. II. Title.

TL685.3 .C5766 2001
623.7'46'068—dc21

                                                                2001031971

RAND is a nonprofit institution that helps improve policy and decisionmaking through research and analysis. RAND® is a registered trademark. RAND's publications do not necessarily reflect the opinions or policies of its research sponsors.

Cover illustration courtesy of Lockheed Martin.

Published 2001 by RAND
1700 Main Street, P.O. Box 2138, Santa Monica, CA 90407-2138
1200 South Hayes Street, Arlington, VA 22202-5050
201 North Craig Street, Suite 102, Pittsburgh, PA 15213
RAND URL: http://www.rand.org/
To order RAND documents or to obtain additional information,
contact Distribution Services: Telephone: (310) 451-7002;
Fax: (310) 451-6915; Email: order@rand.org

The costs of military aircraft are coming under increasing scrutiny in the post–Cold War threat environment because of the decreasing size of the budgets of the military departments, particularly the procurement portions of these budgets. As part of this focus, the Department of Defense (DoD) established a number of studies and cost reduction initiatives during the 1990s to control or reduce the cost of the weapon systems planned, under development, or in production. Under the umbrella of the concept of "Acquisition Reform," such initiatives as Cost as an Independent Variable (CAIV), the Lean Aerospace Initiative (LAI), and the use of integrated product teams (IPTs) were established.

At the same time, manufacturers claimed that the package of new tools and techniques known as "lean production" would enable them to produce new weapons systems at costs below those predicted by historical cost estimating models. Lean production is a manufacturing system deriving from the Japanese Toyota automobile production model, where closely coupled manufacturing systems characterized by very low inventory and first-time quality remove much of the non-value-added work. The application of "lean" as a descriptor of manufacturing activities has many interpretations and varies somewhat from organization to organization. Generally, lean production involves a reconceptualization of the entire production process as a closely interconnected system from which buffers are removed. All the different activities that are part of the production process must be carefully coordinated to maximize the benefits of lean production. The associated organizational and coordination requirements make implementing lean production a difficult and complex endeavor. Liker and Wu (2000) define "lean" as "a philosophy of manufacturing that focuses on delivering the highest-quality product at the lowest cost and on time." A systematic and continuing search for non-value-added activities and sources of waste concentrates the focus on quality and cost. New tools and techniques are incorporated as part of the continual effort to cut costs and improve quality and to enable reduced inventories and other lean practices.

As part of the increased scrutiny of costs, DoD decisionmakers began insisting on better forecasts of weapon systems costs, so cost growth could be minimized. However, DoD cost estimators faced the task of how to assess the impacts of both of these phenomena in their estimates for future aircraft systems. Many of the DoD decisionmakers and some professional cost analysts believed that use of historical cost data as the basis for estimates of future systems was analogous to "trying to drive a car while looking through the rear view mirror." The basic questions were whether the historically derived cost estimating methodologies should be modified and, if so, how to do it.

This report (one of a series on estimating future aircraft costs) was undertaken in Project AIR FORCE's Resource Management Program for the Assistant Secretary of the Air Force (Acquisition) to determine whether current cost estimating tools for new aircraft could be adjusted to account for lean production impacts. It should be of interest to all DoD acquisition personnel. It assesses the extent of lean implementation in the military aircraft industry and claims of savings and offers insights and issues for the government cost estimators to consider when incorporating new production processes into aircraft cost estimates.

Project AIR FORCE

Project AIR FORCE, a division of RAND, is the Air Force federally funded research and development center (FFRDC) for studies and analyses. It provides the Air Force with independent analyses of policy alternatives affecting the development, employment, combat readiness, and support of current and future aerospace forces. Research is performed in four programs: Aerospace Force Development; Manpower, Personnel, and Training; Resource Management; and Strategy and Doctrine.

CONTENTS

FIGURES

TABLES

This report is part of a project responding to a call by the U.S. Air Force to update cost estimating methodologies for new weapons systems—in particular, fighter aircraft. The Air Force was concerned that Cost Estimating Relationships (CERs) based on older aircraft did not adequately reflect the acquisition and manufacturing environment within which a new fighter, such as the Joint Strike Fighter (JSF) would be produced. This report is one of a series, all of which address some aspect of how to incorporate the new DoD acquisition and manufacturing environments into historical cost estimating relationships or methodologies (See Younossi, Graser, and Kennedy, 2001; Lorell and Graser, 2001).

Using the CER methodology for example, the cost of a future aircraft is estimated as a function of its physical or performance characteristics or other program variables, using a series of equations wherein the performance and program variables are inputs, and cost or labor hours are the outputs. To create these equations, actual costs (or labor hours) to produce previous aircraft are collected and used as the dependent variables in statistical regression analysis. Explanatory variables typically include such factors as cumulative production quantity, annual production rate, such aircraft characteristics as weight and speed, and others. The resulting equations are referred to as "cost estimating relationships," or CERs. Obviously, the ability of these equations to forecast future systems costs hinges on how well past performance is a predictor of the future.

Manufacturers and many in DoD contend that because of revolutionary changes in the ways military aircraft are designed and built, aircraft can be produced for lower costs than historical CERs would predict. They claim that new business practices, including the impact of lean manufacturing,[1] will enable significant savings over historical costs. These potential savings from lean manufacturing are of particular interest to the Air Force in the cost-conscious post–Cold War defense environment.

Because of the overlap of claimed savings due to new (post-1990) military aircraft design and manufacturing initiatives (especially for advanced airframe materials), acquisition reform, and lean implementation, RAND research was divided into four studies as follows:

- New fabrication and assembly processes related to advanced airframe materials are addressed in Younossi et al. (2001).

- Government changes in acquisition processes or changes in the relationship between the government and prime DoD contractors (known as "acquisition reform" implementation) are addressed in Lorell and Graser (2001).

- Lean implementation and other initiatives primarily oriented to processes within a prime airframe manufacturer or between these primes and their suppliers will be addressed in this report. To ensure completeness, this report also includes such initiatives as the introduction of technologies that "enable" or enhance lean manufacturing, but which purists might not categorize as lean.

- Propulsion impacts will be addressed in a report currently in work at RAND.

(See Appendix A for a listing of all military aircraft initiatives addressed in the first three of these reports.)

These savings claims by industry and some government officials were assessed using evidence provided during site visits by RAND researchers to all U.S. defense prime aircraft manufacturers, many of their major airframe subcontractors, and a small selection of lower-tier suppliers.

---

[1]The lean manufacturing system is explained in detail in Chapter Two of this report.

This report addresses three questions regarding the adoption of lean manufacturing in the U.S. defense aircraft sector:

- To what extent have U.S. aircraft manufacturers implemented lean practices into their factories and what are the likely savings on military aircraft from this implementation?

- Is there sufficient documented and quantified evidence available from industry to support the notion that these savings should be incorporated into cost estimating methodologies?

- If so, what techniques should be used to modify cost estimating methodologies so estimates of future aircraft costs reflect the latest industry initiatives? Can a taxonomy be established for assigning these savings somehow into the Contractor Cost Data Reporting (CCDR) categories, which are the basic divisions under which actual cost data is collected about DoD aircraft under development or in production?

To briefly summarize the state of the lean implementation in the military aircraft industry in 1998:

- Nearly all of the manufacturers had embraced "lean," as evidenced by the appointment of a Vice President or Director of Lean or of related affordability initiatives, whose main responsibility was implementation of cost savings efforts.

- Nearly all manufacturers had lean pilot projects in operation or planned for the near term.

- All of those manufacturers with pilot projects reported savings on the factory floor from these initial activities.

- None had implemented lean practices from beginning to end of the value stream or even "wall to wall" within the factory.

- Unions and the workforce in nonunionized plants had at least grudgingly accepted lean practices and principles because of the realization that any future job security depended on their companies' abilities to produce affordable military aircraft.

Although anecdotal and pilot project evidence supported the contention that the implementation of lean manufacturing principles could reduce the cost of aircraft, it was impossible to fully assess the claims regarding the magnitude of the effect of lean manufacturing on final aircraft costs because there was limited evidence of thorough, systematic implementation of the lean manufacturing system in any defense aircraft plant affecting its related product. Instead, lean implementation tended to be very localized within particular functions or on pilot projects. Savings from these pilot projects should not be generalized to forming predictions regarding the entire factory floor without further analysis because integrating individual "leaned-out" cells into a smooth continuous-flow production design is a separate and significant effort. The lean enterprise model also incorporates a great deal of change in areas outside the production facility, from engineering to supplier management to plant and corporate administration. Predicting the potential savings available from leaning out these areas cannot be done by generalizing the results from factory production cells.

The bottom-line finding of the report is that no macro adjustments to historical CERs are possible at this time because of the dearth of systematic data collection on the savings being achieved from strictly lean practices. This does not suggest that companies and government officials are not trying hard to reduce weapon system costs through the application of lean principles but that quantifying these savings into the bottom-line cost of systems in CERs must wait a few more years until actual data can be collected and analyzed. In the interim, we suggest that individual lean initiatives be analyzed and baseline cost estimates derived from historical CERs be discretely adjusted for these claimed savings on a case-by-case basis. This methodology is being used on the F-22 program through the Production Cost Reduction Plans (PCRPs).

Readers should be able to take four points away from this document. First, they should get a broad overview of lean manufacturing and understand many of the specifics that go into a lean system. This material has been published (at least in part) in other reports, but it is presented as context and also to introduce lean manufacturing to readers who would like to learn more about it. Other presentations often focus on the automobile or other high-volume industries; this report discusses lean production in the specific context of the manufacture of military aircraft. In addition, we feel that the lean philosophy has more "staying power" than many of the other management philosophies of the recent and not-so-recent past, so cost estimators must be knowledgeable of these principles and their potential impacts on cost as they develop estimates for military aircraft in the future.

Second, the report details the results of industry efforts described to RAND as of 1998 by military aircraft manufacturers. These include specific examples and claimed broad averages of cost savings.

Third, the report discusses the DoD Contractor Cost Data Reporting System and how lean manufacturing savings claims could influence costs in each category of the CCDR System.

Finally, the report discusses where companies need to push harder in lean implementation and what DoD can do to encourage this.

ACKNOWLEDGMENTS

The cooperation and participation of many individuals involved in military and commercial aerospace production, both at the prime contractor and subcontractor level, made this study possible. We have diligently tried to reflect the data and information provided accurately.

We are indebted to Lt Gen Stephen B. Plummer, the USAF Principal Deputy Assistant Secretary for Acquisition, the current project sponsor, General Gregory S. Martin, project sponsor while he was in SAF/AQ, and Lt Gen (Ret) George K. Muellner, the former USAF Principal Deputy for Acquisition, who initiated the project, as well as John Dorsett and Jay Jordan, former and current Technical Directors of the Air Force Cost Analysis Agency, who served as the project monitors. They provided helpful insights throughout the project evolution. Lt Gen Leslie F. Kenne, former Joint Strike Fighter Program Director, was instrumental in opening doors and encouraging contractors to support this project.

We greatly appreciate the time, data, and helpful comments from many individuals at the prime contractors and major subcontractors that participated in this study. Participating contractors included Boeing–Seattle; Boeing–St. Louis (formerly the headquarters of McDonnell Douglas); Boeing–Philadelphia; Boeing–Long Beach; Boeing–Palmdale; Lockheed Martin Aeronautics–Fort Worth; Lockheed Martin Aeronautics–Marietta; Lockheed Martin Aeronautics–Palmdale; Northrop Grumman Integrated Aero Structures–El Segundo; Northrop Grumman Integrated Aero Structures–Dallas; Raytheon Aircraft–Wichita; Bell Helicopter Textron–Fort Worth; and

xix

Sikorsky Helicopters–Bridgeport. Helpful people at each site offered presentations and useful insights, participated in discussions and interviews, and conducted the plant tours at each location. They are unfortunately too numerous to list individually.

Finally, we would like to thank our colleagues, Frank Camm, Sally Sleeper, and Bob Roll, whose comments on the draft report were instrumental in improving the final document. Any remaining errors are due to the incomplete implementation of lean manufacturing principles by the authors.

ABBREVIATIONS

AR   Acquisition Reform

CAD   Computer-Aided Design

CAIV   Cost as an Independent Variable

CAM   Computer-Aided Manufacturing

CNC   Computer numerically controlled

CCDR   Contractor Cost Data Reporting

CER   Cost Estimating Relationship

COTS   Commercial Off-the-Shelf

DFM/A   Design for Manufacturing and Assembly

DSARC   Defense Systems Acquisition Review Council

ECO   Engineering change order

EDI   Electronic Data Interchange

EMD   Engineering and Manufacturing Development

ERP   Enterprise Resource Planning

FOD   Foreign Object Debris or Foreign Object Damage

FPRA   Forward Pricing Rate Agreement

G&A   General and Administrative

HRM   Human resources management

HSM   High-speed machining

IMVP   International Motor Vehicle Program

IPPD   Integrated Product and Process Development
IPT   Integrated product team
JIT   Just in time
JSF   Joint Strike Fighter
LAI   Lean Aerospace Initiative
LC   Learning curve
LTA   Long-term agreement
MIT   Massachusetts Institute of Technology
MRB   Material Review Board
MRP   Material Resource Planning
OJT   On-the-job training
OSD   Office of the Secretary of Defense
PCRP   Production Cost Reduction Plan
PPBS   Planning, Programming, and Budgeting
       System (DoD)
PSM   Purchasing and Supplier Management
QA   Quality assurance
QC   Quality control
SPC   Statistical process control
SPF/DB Super plastic forming/diffusion bonding
T1   Theoretical first aircraft unit cost
TPM   Total Productive Maintenance
TQM   Total Quality Management
USAF   U.S. Air Force
WBS   Work Breakdown Structure
WIP   Work in Process or Work in Progress

Chapter One

INTRODUCTION

A revolution in manufacturing has swept through the United States within the last 10 years, a revolution that has changed the way innovative firms develop and manufacture their products and deal with their customers and suppliers. The aggregate results have been notable, with a 40 percent improvement in manufacturing productivity in the United States between 1989 and 1998 (Weinstein, 1999, pp. B1, B3).

Sources of the improvements that have led to this revolution are many. New technologies are a traditional driver of higher productivity, as improvements in machines and other kinds of tools enable workers to become more efficient. New processes and ways of organizing work have also contributed to productivity improvements over the years, exemplified historically in the introduction of the assembly line and more recently by the explosive expansion in the use of computer technologies. The past decade has seen the introduction of dramatic improvements in technology and manufacturing processes. New computer technologies allow firms to regulate and improve everything from the initial design of their products to the ordering of material to incorporate into the product to the movement of the product through the factory floor. On the factory floor, the movement from batch production to cellular manufacturing has been linked with reduced labor hours, higher quality, lower inventories, lower floor space requirements, and other efficiency improvements. The "lean manufacturing" system offers one systematic strategy for improvement that incorporates many of these new best practices, including those new technologies and best practice techniques and tools.

The military aircraft sector in the United States has to some extent been historically shielded from the pressures that have driven other firms to seek cost reductions through the adoption of such production practices as lean manufacturing. National security considerations and a lengthy Cold War kept service requirements, personnel, and airplane manufacturers more focused on developing the new technology required to stay competitive in the arms race than on cost considerations of weapons systems. These firms also have not faced the same level of foreign competition as commercial industries, because the U.S. Department of Defense (DoD) is essentially required to purchase its weapons from domestic firms. A strong domestic defense industrial base is seen by most as a strategic requirement. Hence no Toyota or other foreign company can realistically expect to make inroads into the defense market, as they have in the U.S. automobile market.

More recently, with the end of the Cold War and increased pressure from Congress and DoD to emphasize affordability, even at the expense of cutting-edge capability, U.S. weapons manufacturers have begun adopting the principles and techniques of lean manufacturing. Several events in particular stand out as drivers of this focus on cost. One is congressional resistance to the high total program costs of the F-22. This has driven Lockheed Martin and Boeing to adopt new practices to control cost growth in an attempt to stay within the congressionally mandated budget limits. The second is the upcoming Joint Strike Fighter (JSF) aircraft production, a program of some 3,000 aircraft. DoD has indicated to the competitors that they need to demonstrate the cost savings from lean manufacturing by defining these practices now, rather than by making vague promises of cost savings at some future date. Furthermore, these two companies as well as others have the incentive to cut costs to get follow-on business on existing programs from both the U.S. government and foreign sales. Foreign governments in particular have a choice in their procurement and will only buy from U.S. arms manufacturers if their prices are competitive in the world market.

This report addresses three questions regarding the adoption of lean manufacturing in the U.S. defense aircraft sector:

- To what extent have U.S. aircraft manufacturers implemented lean production in their factories and what are the likely savings on military aircraft from this implementation?

- Is sufficient documented and quantified evidence available from industry to support the notion that these savings should be incorporated into cost estimating methodologies?

- If so, what techniques should be used to modify cost estimating methodologies so estimates of future aircraft costs reflect the latest industry initiatives? Can a taxonomy be established for assigning these savings somehow into the Contractor Cost Data Reporting (CCDR) categories?

Part I

LEAN MANUFACTURING METHODS OF STUDY

Chapter Two

THE LEAN MANUFACTURING SYSTEM

THE SEARCH FOR PRODUCTIVITY IMPROVEMENTS AND THE GENESIS OF LEAN MANUFACTURING

Over the past 10 years or so, lean manufacturing has been receiving an increasing amount of attention as one source for productivity improvements and cost reductions in manufacturing. Hailed by its proponents as a breakthrough means to analyze and improve production and the factory floor environment, lean manufacturing is a broad collection of principles and practices that can improve corporate performance. The argument is that lean manufacturing offers revolutionary rather than evolutionary efficiency improvements. While lean manufacturing has received a lot of publicity since the term was coined as part of a study analyzing world automobile production, it is very difficult to find a concise definition of the term that describes all aspects of the system. Lean manufacturing is very closely related to Total Quality Management and derives from the Toyota production model. It involves a reconceptualization of the entire production process as a closely interconnected system from which buffers are removed. All the different activities that are part of the production process must be carefully coordinated to maximize the benefits of lean; the associated organizational and coordination requirements make implementing lean production a difficult and complex endeavor.

Liker and Wu (2000) define "lean" as "a philosophy of manufacturing that focuses on delivering the highest-quality product at the lowest cost and on time. It is a system of production that also takes a value stream focus. The 'value stream' consists of all the steps in the process needed to convert raw material into the product the customer desires."

Researchers at the Lean Aerospace Initiative (LAI) at the Massachusetts Institute of Technology describe lean as "adding value by eliminating waste, being responsive to change, focusing on quality, and enhancing the effectiveness of the workforce."[1] Babson (1995, p. 6) summarizes some aspects of a lean facility as follows:

> Inventories in a "lean" plant are taken on a just-in-time basis to minimize handling and expose defective parts before they accumulate in the warehouse; stockpiles of in-process work are also sharply reduced so that defects are immediately exposed at their source, before they fill the plant's repair bays with defective products; "indirect" labor (supervision, inspection, maintenance) is pared and specialized job classifications are reduced or eliminated, replaced by teams of cross-trained production workers who rotate jobs and take on responsibilities for quality control, repair, housekeeping, and preventive maintenance.

A systematic and continuing search for non-value-added activities and sources of waste forces a focus on quality and cost. New tools and techniques are incorporated as part of the continual effort to cut costs and improve quality and to enable reduced inventories and other lean practices.

Although lean manufacturing has its origins in the automobile-manufacturing sector, other industries have adopted the practices to improve their own operations. Womack and Jones (1996) offer several case studies of firms making radically different products, including stretch-wrapping machines, wire management systems and power protection devices, and aircraft engines, among others. Liker (1998) reports improvements for a tannery, a maker of sealing components, a scientific products company, a maker of outdoor cedar products (including birdhouses), a manufacturer of seismic exploration equipment, and companies in the automobile supply chain. Many other adoptions of lean principles have been reported as well,

---

[1]http://lean.mit.edu/public/index.html. LAI is a consortium of industry, government, and academia dedicated to researching the benefits of lean production and propagating lean manufacturing throughout the defense aerospace industry.

although hard quantitative data on proven savings is unfortunately limited.

The search for improvements in production processes is by no means new. The eighteenth century economist Adam Smith is not usually thought of as an industrial engineer. However, his 1776 discussion in *An Inquiry into the Nature and Causes of the Wealth of Nations* regarding the division of labor in the manufacture of pins was one of the first formal examples of how to improve efficiency in production. Rather than having one worker make the pin from start to finish (drawing out the wire, straightening it, cutting it, sharpening it, putting the head on), he suggested that by dividing up the tasks involved in the production of pins and having a different worker perform each separate task, many more pins could be produced in a day. The process of dividing tasks into components and assigning different workers to complete each task was one of the enablers of the efficiency improvements in the industrial revolution, which was also driven by new sources of energy, new types of machine tools, population growth, broader changes in social structure, and many other factors.

The "father of scientific management," Frederick W. Taylor (1911) took a systematic approach to the organization of production. He focused on making workers' movements more efficient, giving them proper tools to do their jobs (e.g.., different shovels to handle different kinds of materials), and organizing work within the workspace to maximize the amount that could get done. Another critical aspect of Taylor's system was the sharp and stated distinction between brainpower of those managers best able to manage how the work actually gets done and the workers that do it. In essence, craft workers were to be "deskilled" (Braverman, 1974) and the analysis of educated engineer managers would replace worker specialist knowledge.

Henry Ford applied scientific management on a grand scale in the production of automobiles. The development of the movable assembly line, coupled with carefully machined interchangeable parts, brought the price of cars down from that of a rich person's toy to a tool for transportation that the middle and working classes could afford. The assembly line marked the transition from "craft" to "mass" production, which remained the dominant model through the 1980s.

Scientific management still drives managers today, as they search for the best way to organize work. Lean production follows this tradition of using careful analysis as a tool in productivity improvements. However, workers in lean factories are considered to be front-line experts on the manufacturing process who can and should participate in the continuing drive to improve productivity.

The improvements offered by Taylor, Ford, and many other thinkers sustained and enabled the growth of the U.S. manufacturing sector for many years and helped the U.S. economy become one of the strongest in the world. In the years after World War II, the United States was undeniably the most important industrial power in the world, with mass production its dominant model.

However, after other countries recovered from the ravages of war and successfully adopted new technologies into their industry, the United States faced more competition in world markets. For example, in the automobile industry, the 1970s and 1980s were marked by the decreasing dominance of U.S. auto manufacturers. Japanese cars became more and more popular, because of the powerful combination of high quality, low price, and better fuel efficiency. Also, Japanese manufacturers were able to take advantage of the oil crisis of the early 1970s by exporting to the United States the compact car models that were the standard in Japan. U.S. automakers were slower to respond with high-quality small cars of their own.

The crisis in U.S. auto manufacturing received increasing attention, as analysts proposed different reasons for the comparative advantage. One popular explanation was cultural, that the Japanese culture as expressed by the homogenous, hardworking people gave Japanese auto manufacturers an advantage based on a dedicated workforce willing to do things that American workers were not, such as going to unpaid meetings after hours to focus on efficiency improvements. Other analysts pointed to particular processes that saved costs, such as just-in-time (JIT) inventory delivery and statistical process control (SPC), which were pervasive in Japan but relatively rare in the United States. Still others pointed to the organization of the workforce, such as quality circles and flexible work categories, as the source of the Japanese advantage. However, U.S. companies adopting these techniques on an individual basis experienced mixed results. High-flying promises of new programs that failed to produce improved performance led to a kind of fatigue, where workers grew increasingly cynical about management commitment and the potential benefits of each successive effort.

In the late 1980s, the International Motor Vehicle Program (IMVP) at the Massachusetts Institute of Technology (MIT) studied automobile manufacturers and compared the United States, Europe, and Japan, to learn the source of the Japanese advantage. The book that was published from this project, *The Machine that Changed the World*, (Womack, Jones, and Roos, 1990) introduced the term "lean manufacturing" to the United States. The authors argued that rather than one or another particular cultural factor, process improvement, or organizational technique being responsible for Japan's success, it was the manufacturing system as a whole. They found that a comprehensive system based on, among other things, maintaining minimal inventories and very high quality, was the basis for the success of the Japanese manufacturers, particularly Toyota. There are many overlaps with the total quality management (TQM) system, although the authors never mention this (Babson, 1995).

Although they popularized the term "lean" to describe the Toyota production system, the authors of the MIT study were not the first to introduce many of these ideas to the West. Indeed, a number of books written prior to the work of Womack and his associates addressed many of the same concepts. Ohno wrote *Toyota Production System: Beyond Large-Scale Production* in 1978 (translated to English in 1988), Shingo's *A Study of the Toyota Production System from an Industrial Engineering Viewpoint* was first translated into English in 1981, Monden wrote *Toyota Production System* in 1983, Goldratt and Cox published the first edition of *The Goal* in 1984, Schonberger penned *World Class Manufacturing* in 1986, and Suzaki wrote *The New Manufacturing Challenge* in 1987. However, *The Machine that Changed the World* was an enormously popular book with managers and was a tremendous sales document for the lean manufacturing system. A second book by two of the same authors, Womack and Jones, *Lean Thinking* (1996), has offered another take on lean manufacturing, and provides examples of companies[2] outside the automobile sector that had successfully adopted the system.

---

[2]Liker's (1998) edited volume offers further examples of lean producers.

OVERVIEW OF THE LEAN MANUFACTURING SYSTEM

Proponents of the lean system claim that it offers the potential for nothing less than revolutionary improvements in performance and cost. Womack et al. (1990) claim that with the entire system in place, production will involve "one-half the human effort in factory, one-half the manufacturing space, one-half the investment tools, one-half the engineering hours, one-half the time to develop new products." The authors also insist that unless the entire group of practices is adopted as a system, performance improvements will be negligible.

Japanese automobile manufacturers achieved high quality and low costs by removing buffers and impediments from the system, hence the term "lean." Eliminating excess inventory, for example, drives closer linkages between assemblers and suppliers, reshapes the factory floor, forces greater attention to first-time quality, and so on. Excess inventory means that manufacturing mistakes or broken equipment will not halt production because downstream processes can draw on inventories to keep going while the mistakes are remedied or the equipment is fixed. However, excess inventory costs money and can hide production problems that lead to greater problems later on. Mass production allows for excess inventory to provide a buffer against mistakes, while lean manufacturing aims to eliminate mistakes and hence the need for costly buffers. Removing inventory buffers requires very tightly coupled processes that closely link different functions within the organization. Further, Womack et al. have contended that the lean system must be adopted wholesale to see improvements. The synergies from applying lean to different areas of the manufacturing process are so significant that new processes cannot be properly understood alone or adopted singly. Such piecemeal efforts could only result in small improvements at best, a fraction of what full-scale implementation would offer.

The practices involve improvements on the manufacturing floor, in supplier management, in inventory management, in design and development, in human resources, and so forth. Attention to quality and flow drives costs down throughout the production process, from the design phase through final delivery to the customer. The authors of *The Machine that Changed the World* take a functional approach to lean processes in the plant and then make the connections across the different functions. In their construct, beginning in the design stage, products are developed to meet customer needs and to be easy to produce out of readily available components. This process requires the input of experts from all different areas on integrated product teams (IPTs).

On the factory floor, components of the product are manufactured one at a time ("single piece flow") in dedicated areas ("cells"). Attention is paid to decreasing setup times and improving first-time quality. Careful inventory management involving minimal or nonexistent inventory stocks keeps costs down, reduces required floor space, and drives the attention to first-time quality so that defects do not halt the flow of production. Similarly, close partnering relationships with suppliers contribute to lower costs and higher quality as suppliers deliver perfect parts and assemblies to the factory floor right before they are needed and continuously work to improve their own quality and reduce their costs. A trained and flexible workforce can play a role in continuous improvement and quality enhancement in a structure that allows workers to have jobs that are comparatively enriched. Close links with customers make sure their needs are met and final product delivery occurs when required. Overhead and other indirect costs are carefully managed as well, with attention paid to which procedures truly add value and which are not necessary (i.e., the collection of data for metrics that are never used), and levels of management structure are kept to a minimum.

In their second book on the topic, *Lean Thinking*, Womack and Jones (1996) depart from a specifically functional approach and offer a more general way of understanding lean manufacturing. They outline the five principles of the system as follows: (1) defining value for each product, (2) eliminating all unnecessary steps in every value stream, (3) making value flow, (4) knowing that the customer pulls all activity, and (5) pursuing perfection continuously. The five principles are laid out in some detail here because they contribute to the understanding of lean manufacturing throughout the plant. Taken together, these principles may offer powerful performance enhancements.

However, while companies can incorporate these principles in their business practices, they often do not correspond to the functional divisions within companies, which may be separately managed and about which data are separately collected. In addition, a practice that could help the plant get leaner as a whole may actually reduce the efficiency in one department. This point is relevant to defense production, where government regulations require the collection and reporting of costs in particular categories and where an increase in one category is not necessarily clearly linked to a decrease in another and so may look like inefficient cost growth rather than an expense related to overall performance improvement.

The first task in lean implementation is identifying what *value* the product has and what the value stream looks like. A fighter aircraft has value to its ultimate customer, the U.S. government (as a proxy for U.S. citizens) in its contribution to defense. The Joint Strike Fighter and F-22 Raptor offer different types of value to the government according to their different defense roles. Value is defined "in terms of specific products with specific capabilities offered at specific prices through a dialogue with specific customers" (Womack and Jones, 1996, p. 19).

Once value is specified, the next step is to determine the *value stream*. Manufacturers need to understand every step in the aircraft's construction, that is to say, the value stream, to produce it efficiently. Then, a manufacturer should continually look for unnecessary steps and other forms of waste (*muda* in Japanese) and reduce or eliminate this waste. For example, production engineers can measure distance traveled (either by the part or by the workers involved) in the creation of a part and search for ways to reduce it.

The third lean principle involves making value *flow* through the plant. Components of the final product should flow smoothly through the plant, going from station to station without a lot of waiting time in between. The traditional approach to this is manufacturing plants organized by task. For example, there would be dedicated cutting areas, dedicated drilling areas, and so forth. Parts would be brought to the area, stored until the machines were free, worked on, and then moved onto the area where the next process would take place. Management focus tended to be on the efficiency of the work station (for example in machine utilization rates) rather than product value flow. Another aspect of flow involves a continuing search for and analysis of bottlenecks in the production process. These occur when one operation slows the critical path of the product as it moves through the factory, thereby increasing total cycle time of production. This may be because of insufficient machine capacity, high tool changeover times, and so forth. As each bottleneck is solved, a new one is almost always identified, by definition, until the factory is completely "leaned" out. In the Toyota model, the process for identifying bottlenecks involves continuously speeding up the line and looking for points where the work is not getting done in the allotted time. Devoting resources to alleviate those stress points means the production line can run at a higher speed. The analysis of bottlenecks, while an important feature of the lean production system, is considerably more difficult outside the context of a traditional assembly line. Without a smooth yet rapid production flow, the bottlenecks may be invisible. Cellular layout of the plant, combined with a consistent, even production pacing, makes bottlenecks more obvious and allows their root causes to be identified and corrected.

The fourth principle is knowing that the customer *pulls* all activity. In short, this means that production should be tied to demand; no products should be built until downstream demand for them occurs. Pull production involves considerable collaboration with customers, to know what they require and when they require it, and with suppliers, to make sure their inputs are supplied at the appropriate time. Ironically, one of the strengths of the DoD and congressional budget processes is that they force conformance to this lean principle because defense manufacturers build aircraft only when ordered, after the money has been appropriated by Congress.

The constant pursuit of *perfection* is the fifth principle of lean thinking. Companies dedicated to lean manufacturing constantly search for ways to improve their efficiencies, to cut costs, and to improve the quality of their products. A number of tools can be drawn on. For example, *kaizen* events[3] are short (usually about a week) projects that study particular processes and look for low-cost ways for improvement. One example provided by Womack and Jones in *Lean Thinking* is of a series of *kaizen* events to improve the manufacture

---

[3]These are also known as "action workouts." Technically, the term *kaizen* represents a broad approach that favors continuous improvement (Imai, 1986) but has been adopted in the United States as a descriptor for these short-term improvement exercises.

of vibration dampers at a Freudenberg-NOK factory in Indiana. Each event over a three-year period led to significant improvements. The question of why the company did not get it right the first time is misguided, since "perfection" must be striven for continually but can never really be reached, because further potential improvements in cost or quality always exist.

These five principles do not stand alone. Rather, there is considerable overlap in what they involve. For example, without near-perfect production, including very high-quality shipments received from suppliers, value cannot flow smoothly through the plant. Out-of-control processes will create problems. The search for waste and wasteful processes can help improve the quality of products and assist in the search for perfection, just as efforts toward continuous improvement will help identify waste. Both of these principles help the product (value) flow more smoothly through the plant.

As described, a major guiding principle of lean manufacturing is the removal of various forms of waste from the manufacturing process. For example, one major source of waste is the inefficient movement of parts throughout the factory. The entire time the part is in the plant, being moved from place to place and not being worked on, is classified as waste. Suzaki (1987, p. 12) reports seven types of waste identified at Toyota: waste from overproduction, waste of waiting time, transportation waste, processing waste, inventory waste, waste of motion, and waste from product defects. He adds an eighth type: the waste of underutilized people's skills and capabilities (p. 208). Implementation of lean manufacturing requires the identification and removal of these forms of waste but, more important, requires making the ongoing identification of this waste a critical activity. This underlies attempts at *continuous improvement.*

COMPLEXITIES AND CHALLENGES

Lean manufacturing is relatively easy to simplify, as it generally appears in most articles and books, including this one. In small plants, producing simple products, it may be easy to identify all the areas that must be changed to create a lean system. However, a single factory tour in a more complex industry, such as aircraft production, will make the analyst realize the challenges and complexities of any large-scale organizational changes, such as those presented by the implementation of lean manufacturing.

A related complexity arises from how lean principles cut across the whole enterprise but must be disaggregated and flowed down to different functional areas within organizations to get work done. Proper supplier management, inventory management, design and development, human resources,[4] and manufacturing operations are critical to lean production, but responsibility for managing these tasks are found in different departments throughout the firm. Implementing a truly lean system across a firm requires an intensive effort to tightly couple related tasks across functional departments. And lean implementation in different functional areas is closely related. For example, issues of concern during design and development can directly affect the manufacturing process, such as the ease of assembling parts into the final configuration. Just-in-time delivery requires the development of close ties with suppliers, keeps inventory low, and has significant effects on the factory floor. Truly lean manufacturing occurs when functions are tightly coupled across the organization to ensure that relevant issues for other functions are raised within each individual function.

Another set of complexities of lean manufacturing regards the cross-functional nature of many of the lean best practices in manufacturing plants.

These complexities make capturing cost improvements related to any one lean initiative or new lean best practice very difficult. Figure 2.1 shows the interrelationships of the various activities needed to manufacture a product and how all must be managed to improve overall operating efficiency.

It is not necessarily a given, in spite of what its proponents suggest, that lean production is the best way to do business. It offers a powerful package, but uncritically accepting all lean tenets, originally

---

[4]Note the enormous volume of academic literature on organizational theory that looks at the role and behavior of individuals in organizations. Scott's (1998) review of the organizational literature is an excellent resource for understanding these questions. Although some of this material is relevant to the discussions on lean manufacturing, providing a full accounting of it is beyond the scope of this document.

RAND*MR1325-2.1*

Design and Development

- Integrated Product and Process Development
- Integrated product teams
- Computer-aided design
- Attention to lean design principles (e.g., unitization, part count reduction)
- Design For Manufacturing and Assembly (DFM/A)
- Design for lean tooling

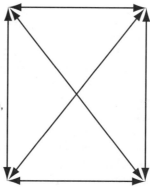

Purchasing and Supplier

- Partnerships with suppliers
- Supplier involvement in design
- Gainsharing
- Suppliers and customers linked digitally (CAD, delivery schedules, invoices and payment, etc.)

Manufacturing

- Pull/cellular system
- Reduced inventories
- First-time quality
- Continuous improvement

Human Resources

- Trained, flexible, empowered workforce
- Team participation
- Touch labor contribution to identification, removal of costs, quality problems

Figure 2.1—Lean Production Is an Enterprise Approach: Linked Functions Affect One Another

based on a high-volume industry, could lead to problems in low-volume situations. For example, aircraft manufacturing involves the production of relatively low volumes over a number of years. Some parts become obsolete and may be unavailable for the entire production run unless purchased at the beginning. This runs directly counter to JIT delivery of parts and is a particular danger in sectors characterized by rapid technological change, such as avionics. (However, Spear and Bowen [1999] report that at Toyota there is flexibility about the "no inventory" rule depending on circumstances.) Also, trade studies must be done to compare the costs of buying a couple of units a year with the costs of buying all required units up front when there are possibilities of volume discounts.

Another concern raised by researchers on human resources and industrial relations issues is the danger that lean production may be just another way to stress workers into producing "more with less," without giving them true input into how the work is done. Various critics have made similar points, including Rinehart, Huxley, and Robertson (1997); Berggren (1992); and several authors in Babson's (1995) edited volume. Proponents of the lean system counter that making workers work harder without giving them the means to work smarter is not truly lean and that lean production is impossible without an empowered and participating workforce.

Finally, no discussion of the possibility of efficiency improvements of 25 percent or more in an industry with limited competitive pressures would be complete without reference to Leibenstein's *X-Efficiency* (1966). Leibenstein argues that traditional measures of allocative inefficiency are inadequate to understand the scope of the costs of monopoly power. (While the defense aircraft industry does have more than one competitor and hence is not a monopoly in the fullest sense of the word, once a contract is awarded to a particular company, it becomes the only supplier of that aircraft and in that sense develops monopoly power.) In an extremely condensed form, the argument is that firms without competition lose incentives to search for normal operating efficiencies in their production and hence lag behind what the most competitive firms can do. They do not need to match the cost and quality improvements of competitors and so do not make the investments required to improve.

This behavior is fostered by the normal DoD contract negotiations for follow-on lots where price is a function of the costs of previous lots plus an allowance for profit. This raises the question of whether potential savings from lean production in the aircraft sector stem from truly innovative ways of doing business or merely from the adoption of evolutionary improvements that the firms just had not bothered to implement until pressured. Developing a thorough answer to this question is outside the scope of this report, however. The focus here is not to judge why opportunities for improvement exist but whether they exist, what savings are possible, and what goals are being achieved.

Lean Implementation in the Military Aircraft Industry

The potential for lean methods to improve efficiency, quality, and cost was not lost on USAF officials or the military aircraft industry. The LAI was born out of practicality and necessity as declining defense procurement budgets collided with military industrial over-capacity, prompting a demand for "cheaper, faster, and better" products. "The initiative was formally launched in 1993 when leaders from the U.S. Air Force, the Massachusetts Institute of Technology, labor unions, and defense aerospace businesses forged a trailblazing partnership to revolutionize the industry, reinvigorate the workplace, and reinvest in America using a philosophy called 'lean.'"[5]

Military aircraft companies have many features that distinguish them from nondefense firms in how they operate and manufacture products for their major and often only customer, the Department of Defense. These differences pose the question as to whether the same kinds of improvements experienced by commercially oriented firms can be implemented by DoD aircraft manufacturers. The first difference is the quantities produced each year. Even at its peak planned production, the JSF will roll off the line at a rate of just over 200 aircraft per year. In contrast, a single Toyota plant in Georgetown, Kentucky, has the capacity to produce 500,000 vehicles a year.[6] Secondly, commercial firms put their own funds at risk to develop and market a new product and either enjoy the profits to be made from a widely sold product or suffer the financial consequences for an unpopular product. In the military aircraft market, DoD pays for the development of the system and pays profit on the costs incurred during development. Although the companies' profit prospects are limited during production, their likelihood of loss is also practically nonexistent. Third, the approval process for a military aircraft development or production is complicated and time-consuming, with many participants involved in not only the initial acquisition decision but also subsequent funding decisions each year by military department and officials in the Office of the Secretary of Defense, as well as Congress. Thus, the ability to bring products to market quickly is hampered by the many government decision processes.

Finally, prices for military aircraft production are based on negotiated values, which are derived from assessing a manufacturer's costs

---

[5]Lean Aerospace Initiative Web page (http://web.mit.edu/lean/).

[6]Toyota Web page (http://www.toyota.com/html/about/opertions/manufacturing/manu-locations/tmmk.html).

and allowing a reasonable profit as a percentage of those costs. This is where cost analysis has come into its own as an activity.

It became clear during the research for this report that defense firms tend to cut costs when competitive forces or pressures from their customers compel them to look for efficiencies. In the normal defense environment, with prices linked to costs incurred, the incentive to reduce costs to be able to enjoy higher profits does not exist as it does in a commercial market where price and cost are not as directly linked. Reduced costs in the DoD context can result in lower profits. Indeed, more than one company claimed that it was pressure from the JSF Program Office for the demonstration of real cost savings that provided the impetus to start efforts at improving efficiency by implementing lean manufacturing. The imposition of a cost cap by Congress on the F-22 provided a strong incentive to reduce and control expenses.

This points out the unmistakable distinction between current programs and potential programs, such as the JSF. Achieving cost reductions on an existing production program can be very difficult— a government agency may suffer as much or more from a canceled program as the defense contractor, so its power to exert pressure on costs through the threat of program cancellation may be limited. Without a tradition of reliable partnering with contractors in a joint effort to improve costs and profits, DoD lacks significant experience and resources to effectively encourage change on existing programs. In addition, once an aircraft design is agreed on, future changes, even for more affordable manufacturing, can require significant up-front investments that may not earn a return for several years and cannot be justified in a budget environment that discourages even multiyear commitments for major defense purchases. On future production programs, the government can threaten cancellation or competition if contractors do not keep their costs in line. However, once the procurement decision is made, cost-based contracts offer less incentive for contractors to pay close attention to costs, as long as program costs do not become high enough to jeopardize a weapon system's very existence.

The discussion of how to encourage contractors to adopt best practices grows out of historical evidence showing that effectively generating change is extremely difficult. Merely learning about the potential benefits of lean manufacturing through participation in a voluntary consortium, such as the Lean Aerospace Initiative, which disseminated lean lessons and techniques, proved to be insufficient to encourage companies to take the necessary but difficult steps toward broad organizational change. This frustration was expressed by Jacques Gansler, Under Secretary of Defense (Acquisition, Technology, and Logistics) when he said:

> I had hoped that, with five years of "lean" research under your belt, we would have begun to see some significant impact on the "top lines" of our defense programs, i.e., the overall costs and schedules for weapons systems. I am sure you agree that your successes in specific elements of the production process must be extended and accelerated to all our programs and—most important—that we begin to see quantifiable data demonstrating the benefits of the "lean" approach at the weapon system level. So far, we just haven't been able to produce such data. (Gansler, 1999.)

Complete implementation of the lean manufacturing system involves considerable organizational change. Aerospace manufacturers have shown that they can take the first steps, but they have not totally transformed themselves. Organizational change of any sort is a long and difficult process, and a transition to lean practices involves cultural and process transformations throughout the entire organization. Successful pilot projects limited to a few cells on the factory floor do not provide sufficient proof that this larger-scale change will occur.

Continuing interest, pressure, and/or incentives from the government for process improvements at manufacturers is required to keep their management focused on continuous improvement and could, over time, result in lower costs and higher-quality products. Without such actions by DoD, a very real danger exists that aerospace manufacturers will fail to take either the initial or follow-on actions required by the continuous process improvement focus of lean manufacturing. The next chapter will address how the military aircraft manufacturers have begun to implement lean principles in their companies.

Chapter Three

DATA AND METHODS

Data collection for this report occurred in several stages. The first step involved reviewing literature on new manufacturing methods. The authors reviewed a number of books and articles to develop a framework of lean principles. That in turn drove interview/survey questions, which were sent to manufacturers of aircraft and major subsystems (see Appendix B for questions). Site visits to these companies were made in the summer and fall of 1998, and data were collected on the extent of lean implementation and on cost savings from lean efforts.

In the first stage, an extensive search of publicly available databases was conducted on keywords relating to lean manufacturing. Abstracts of all articles published between 1990 and 1998 were collected. The sheer number (several hundred) of sources made a complete review of all of these articles impossible. Based on the abstracts, articles that offered promise of specifics on performance improvements were collected and assessed. Some offer useful information on lean performance improvements and will be described below. A number of books on lean manufacturing and the Japanese Toyota production model were also collected, including ones published before the term "lean manufacturing" really took hold. Using these books and the articles, a framework of what lean manufacturing involves was developed and is used as a benchmark against which lean implementation was assessed.

After the literature search was completed, a questionnaire was developed to gather details on lean implementation at the participating government organizations and aircraft manufacturers and their suppliers. This questionnaire was sent to a number of sites in advance of RAND's visits. During the site visits, company representatives gave presentations and offered written documentation detailing the answers to the questions. They also provided tours of their factories where lean projects were in operation or had been planned.

The data provided by the companies during the visits were assessed for two purposes. The first was to determine the extent of lean implementation at the sites. To that end, a number of questions were asked that were not directly cost related. The second purpose was an analysis of the data to determine the actual savings the aircraft manufacturers experienced through the implementation of lean production rather than promised or expected savings from future implementation.

The prime contractors and major subcontractors participating in this study were Boeing–Seattle; Boeing–St. Louis; Boeing–Philadelphia; Boeing–Long Beach; Boeing–Palmdale; Lockheed Martin Aeronautics–Fort Worth; Lockheed Martin Aeronautics–Marietta; Lockheed Martin Aeronautics–Palmdale; Northrop Grumman Integrated Aero Structures–El Segundo; Northrop Grumman Integrated Aero Structures–Dallas; Raytheon Aircraft–Wichita; Bell Helicopter Textron–Fort Worth; and Sikorsky Helicopters–Bridgeport.

Note that not all questions were completely answered at any site. How plants responded to the questionnaire varied considerably, both in level of detail on particular questions and as to what questions were answered at all. In this document, the number of data points underlying each overall average performance improvement is given.

One methodological limitation of the literature review and data collection is that only good news tends to be publicized. Although a great many articles on lean manufacturing were reviewed, not one mentioned significant problems with implementation or instances where productivity went down, even temporarily. Similarly, in their formal presentations, companies only offered cases in which lean implementation went smoothly and offered performance improvements. Private conversations with aircraft industry executives in other settings and outside the formal presentations revealed a more mixed story, however. Quietly, people reported cases where cellular production had been tried and abandoned, where IPTs faced insurmountable obstacles from powerful functional organizations, and where the operators were not given the training and support they needed. Lean implementation in aerospace has not been an unequivocal success story. One insight is that while the lean production model does offer the potential for performance enhancements, these improvements will be exaggerated if only positive results are reported. Furthermore, the difficulties of effective lean implementation should not be underestimated.

A related problem is that among the many works that lay out best practices that should be adopted for maximum efficiency, far less published evidence details actual improvements backed up by real savings to end-product prices. The metrics most often reported are reduced floor space and cycle times. Specifics of cost reduction are reported infrequently, while the same few companies receive press repeatedly (i.e., Lantech, Freudenberg-NOK, Wiremold). The lack of specifics is not a journalistic flaw, however. Rather, it is a result of the propensity of companies to keep proprietary cost information private, to avoid giving strategic advantage to suppliers, competitors, and customers.

Another issue in data collection relates to the consolidation of the industry during the past few years. An attempt was made to collect some historical information from the plants to put their current position in better context. For example, supplier consolidation initiatives can be quantified by knowing how many suppliers supported the company in the past and how many support it today. However, the considerable restructuring of the industry that took place in the 1990s means that the relevant data may not exist or may be of questionable accuracy. Hence, the development of a deep historical context within which to place recent attempts at lean implementation was not possible.

The companies that participated in this study were at different points on the road to complete implementation of a lean system across their operations. For the purposes of this report, it would be premature to look at cost savings in a mutually exclusive context of whether the company was lean or nonlean. The aerospace plants visited were for the most part taking serious action to improve their operations. Reported cost savings should be considered improvements from initial lean implementation. This leaves open the possibility that aerospace companies can further improve their performance if they follow the lean concept of continuous improvement.

Womack et al. (1990) contend that one and only one lean manufacturing system exists. Indeed, certain basic precepts underlie its structure, including a consistent focus on improvement throughout the enterprise. However, lean manufacturing can be conducted in a number of ways on the factory floor. There may or may not be one best way. We saw a number of different approaches, tools, techniques, and so forth. It should be noted that adoption of all specific lean best practices is not required for lean implementation and also that two competing lean best practices may enhance performance in different ways. Cost trade-offs must also be analyzed, even when lean implementation is involved. The important point is to determine and focus on the initiatives that have the highest net impact on the *total* weapon system cost, not just those with the largest localized activity percentage reductions.

REPORTING RESULTS: ACCOUNTING FOR SAVINGS FROM LEAN PROCESSES IN DEFENSE MANUFACTURING

If lean manufacturing is thoroughly implemented and proponents of the lean system have accurately represented its potential, savings should show up in the bottom-line price that the government pays for aircraft. Lean manufacturing offers the commercial-world "target pricing" model as a method of setting prices. The model suggests that companies determine the competitive price they would like to charge for their product and work backward through the value stream to determine cost targets for various components of the final product. Careful attention is paid to in-house costs to minimize the prime manufacturer's portion of the cost. Primes use the mechanism of close relationships with their subcontractors and suppliers to help them reduce their prices to the prime contractor and still make their profits.

On large weapons systems, the government normally uses a different method of determining how much it will pay for what it buys, the

cost-plus method.[1] Here, all the different costs to produce the aircraft are estimated, and a percentage for profit is added on top. The
total price is then negotiated with the prime but is still based primarily on projected costs. Successive lot prices are normally based on
the actual costs incurred in producing previous lots, plus profit. This
traditionally has provided a powerful disincentive for manufacturers
to reduce their cost structure because a percentage profit on a
reduced cost structure will yield smaller profits. (It is not the purpose of this report to discuss the causes and consequences of cost-
based contracting, however.) The cost-based method depends on
contractors accurately collecting and reporting their costs. To
ensure the collection of data in a consistent and comparable manner
across programs, the government has created the CCDR system,
which requires contractors to report specifics on different components of cost.

The CCDR System

Government regulations require the collection of specific components of cost for an aircraft development or a particular lot or block
of aircraft production. The CCDR system was developed in the early
1970s. The government's goals in the development of this system
were threefold:

> The main thrust of CCDR is to assist all DOD Components in (1)
> preparing cost estimates for major system acquisitions reviewed by
> the Defense Systems Acquisition Review Council (DSARC) at each
> program decision milestone, (2) developing independent Govern-
> ment cost estimates in support of cost and price analyses and con-
> tract negotiations, and (3) tracking contractor's negotiated cost.
> (OASD, 1999.)

One of the strengths of CCDR is its attempt at standardizing categories of cost so that data can be collected systematically and the
costs of different programs can be compared on a more detailed
level. Cost data reporting elements include engineering, tooling,

---

[1]There is more room for negotiation and a focus on containing costs during the
development stage of a program, where trade-offs between cost and performance can
be made (a process known as Cost as an Independent Variable, or CAIV).

quality control, manufacturing, purchased equipment, material overhead, other costs, general overhead, and subcontract costs. The CCDR manual has specific instructions and many subcategories for classifying costs in reports to the government. In the interest of brevity and to address the impact of lean at a higher level, we have used six broad categories from the CCDR instructions to provide a general portrayal of lean impacts. These six categories are engineering, tooling, quality control, manufacturing, materials and purchased parts, and overhead and general and administrative (G&A) costs, which are treated as one category.

Each of these CCDR categories is treated in a separate chapter. These chapters feature descriptions of the type of effort contained in the category and how lean manufacturing implementation could affect those efforts. Each chapter also provides some specifics of the lean initiatives of different defense aircraft manufacturers and what savings were reported. An additional chapter on lean lessons for managing the workforce is included because worker involvement is critical to the lean system. (However, labor costs are actually captured in the other CCDR categories.)

The defense industry thus presents an additional challenge for lean implementation. If not focused and managed properly, functional data collection can impede the lean approach that explicitly links the overall goal of cost reduction in all of the different functions of the firm. Specific lean initiatives often cross these functional boundaries as well and could result in additional costs incurred in one functional area that reduce the costs in other areas by an even greater amount. Nonetheless, if lean is truly implemented, total weapons system costs should reflect these savings.

Part II

INCORPORATING LEAN INTO COST ESTIMATES
USING CCDR CATEGORIES

Chapter Four

ENGINEERING

INTRODUCTION

In this chapter, we describe in depth the processes and tools that enable lean design, and offer specific examples from the companies that participated in the study. We discuss the mixed evidence of savings from lean design and development and suggest caution in assigning responsibility for outcomes to lean techniques or to any other tools or production processes when government requirements are such a major driver of cost and schedule. The definition of "engineering" in the CCDR Manual can be found in Appendix C.

If lean production is to be successfully implemented, it must start with the engineering function. Design and development conducted in accordance with lean principles should offer payoffs throughout the life of the product, in improved producibility and quality and reduced cost. IPTs are the traditional mechanism by which these inputs are collected. Computer-aided design has become a universal tool that enables lean production in a number of ways.

Companies collect and report total engineering hours as a separate and distinct cost category as part of the government CCDR data-collecting requirement. According to lean principles, however, engineering is intrinsically linked to other functions in the firm, whose costs are collected in other cost categories. An important foundation of the entire lean production system is ensuring that the perspectives of all functions are incorporated in the earliest stages of design. Hence, an investment in engineering to reduce costs of manufacturing will show an increased engineering cost, which may be viewed as a negative if considered without respect to any larger context. Unless the linkage is specifically made, the manufacturer may end up looking like its engineering costs are out of control. With that caveat in mind, there are a number of important aspects to engineering in the lean manufacturing system.

DESIGN ENGINEERING

The first step in the creation of any product is the design phase. Before the benefits of sharing information were widely appreciated, design engineers would be situated remote from the manufacturing facilities, creating their aircraft designs in a rarefied atmosphere, dedicated to advanced concepts rather than practical considerations, like ease of manufacturability.[1] This corresponds to the overall division of the firm into functional departments rather than into teams of experts with different functional backgrounds working together on particular products—the organizational structure suggested by lean manufacturing. When the designers finished their work, they would provide their design to the manufacturing department to have the tooling built and the production line started.

The problems inherent in this approach are legion. Primarily, it does not integrate the many kinds of knowledge possessed across the plant and by partners of the company. Tooling designers may find that particular tools required by the design concept are difficult to build or excessively expensive. Manufacturing engineers may find that actually assembling the parts in the product is very difficult. Purchasing managers may not be able to procure particular parts or materials easily and may have insight on whether suppliers of a certain technology are more or less reliable than suppliers of a substitutable technology. Customer requirements may have changed during the design phase, and the final design may no longer fill these requirements.

A second problem with the traditional design method is the high cycle times. Waiting until the final design is "thrown over the wall" to the other functions means that the rest of the plant cannot get a head start on making their contribution, which lengthens the cycle time between initial product conception and final finished product.

---

[1]This is a "straw-man" worst-case scenario.

Procuring certain items like forgings and castings requires significant lead time; if purchasers have tentative designs, they can start the process and send their design quickly to suppliers who can assess the cost and "manufacturability" of the part and offer suggestions to reduce costs or improve manufacturability. New tools may have to be procured (another potential bottleneck) and employees may need to be trained to use them. Insufficient attention paid to manufacturability by design engineers means lengthy delays as manufacturing engineers develop workarounds or the design is iterated.

The lean manufacturing model attempts to eliminate these problems by taking a different approach. All key internal and external stakeholders are represented on design teams at the beginning of the design period so that they can provide their input early. With a process aimed at ensuring manufacturability using reasonably priced tools tied more directly into what the customer wants and drawing on the particular skills of suppliers, firms should be able to reduce the total cycle time to get a finished product to the customer while increasing the quality and marketability of the product. For example, in the U.S. automobile industry, shortened cycle time for product development is one outcome of the lean manufacturing system that enabled manufacturers to compete better with Japanese carmakers. The product development cycle for Chrysler's LH car series (introduced in 1992) was 39 months, using an in-house technology staff of 740. By contrast, the K-car, from the early 1980s, had 2,000 people on the technology staff and took 54 months (Klier, 1993).

Incorporating lean manufacturing concepts into the design phase can reduce costs of the product during its entire life. Designing for lean methods initially is simpler than reworking approved designs and manufacturing processes later on, in particular if expensive and time-consuming testing and regulatory approval is required for change, as in aircraft production. Currently, two major lean tools can be used during the design phase to improve quality and reduce costs. These are Integrated Product and Process Development (IPPD) using IPTs and CAD.

IPPD and IPTs

IPPD is the generic name for product development activities that incorporate a wide range of perspectives from across the organization. The primary enablers of IPPD are IPTs, the original lean tool for incorporating the knowledge of customers, of suppliers, of operators, of manufacturing engineers, and so forth into the design process to make products that are easier and less expensive to manufacture and that best serve the customers' needs. Cost and performance objectives drive the activities of the participants to work toward the best solution possible.

> Once on a team, the role of an IPT member changes from that of a member of a particular functional organization, who focuses on a given discipline, to that of a team member, who focuses on a product and its associated processes. Each individual should offer his/her expertise to the team as well as understand and respect the expertise available from other members of the team. Team members work together to achieve the team's objectives. (OUSD/A&T, 1996.)

The military aircraft industry has long enjoyed a great deal of input from its principal customer, the U.S. government. More recently, formal IPTs have tried to incorporate skills, knowledge, and requirements of all relevant functions and external participants into the design process. The perceived benefits of IPTs are so great that DoD mandated their use for acquisition programs in 1995 (OUSD/A&T, 1995). Perhaps because of the regulatory requirement, or perhaps because IPTs are a lean practice, all the manufacturers surveyed as part of this research used IPTs for aircraft design activities.

A significant amount of research has been conducted on team structures within organizations (e.g., Katzenbach and Smith, 1993). Issues include identifying and empowering the appropriate members, selecting a suitable leader, frequency of meetings, physical locations of team members, and so forth. A range of opinion exists on how best to staff and organize these teams, issues beyond the scope of this research. In this research, questions about specific team structures were not asked, but data presented indicate that the aircraft manufacturers used different types of team structures. Insufficient data were made available to assess whether one or another of the arrangements was associated with better outcomes. In reality, IPTs must be tailored to the weapons system, manufacturers, and the customers, so a "one size fits all" approach is bound to fail.

During the RAND interviews, contractors universally agreed that IPTs are useful, although some real questions arose about their cost effectiveness. The general perception is that IPTs involve more up-front investment in work-years than do traditional design arrangements. The costs are driven by the requirement of developing new organizational structures. Incorporating the perspectives of a wide range of stakeholders early in the process means that the costs of IPT participation by people from a wide range of functions are incurred early. Instead of funding product design early and manufacturing design later on, both must be funded early in the program. There is also a question of workload intensity of the members of IPTs. Early on, team members from some functions will have a significantly larger workload than other IPT members. Later, these roles may be reversed. But to be successful, all members must be full participants throughout the IPT life cycle.

The hope is that this early investment will result in lower production costs, better products, and shorter product development times. For example, incorporating manufacturing engineers' insights early in the process means that the product as designed should be easier or less expensive to build. The development of a manufacturing plan can be done concomitantly with the development of the actual product design. As IPTs are a relatively new design construction, however, the data are not yet available to support any long-term cost savings, or even whether the up-front IPT investment was offset by lower manufacturing costs for early units. As far as cycle time, in the military aircraft business, the customer often drives the development cycle, which can be stretched out as a result of political and funding decisions as much as because of problems encountered during the actual development activities.

Another way to get a lower-cost product is to incorporate the customers' perspectives during the design process and offer feedback to the customer, particularly on the cost of requirements. If customers know approximately how much an additional operational requirement that "expands the performance envelope" will cost, they will be able to perform cost-benefit trade-offs much earlier. Slight increases in performance that drive extraordinary increases in cost need to be discovered and addressed during the development of overall system requirements. One company offered a telling example regarding cockpit displays. A pilot was shown two different screens and asked to choose between them. One was about eight inches diagonally, the other was larger, about 10 inches on the diagonal. The pilot preferred the larger screen, which drove the requirement to the manufacturer. The pilot was never told that the smaller screen was available as a commercial item and was approximately one-sixth the cost of the larger, unique display. A two-way exchange of information could have allowed for an intelligent trade-off between desirability and cost, perhaps without a significant loss of performance. This phenomenon is addressed by the DoD philosophy of CAIV.

The widespread use of IPTs in the defense aircraft industry should mean that all contractors would be able to provide insight into the benefits and problems of IPTs, and what factors make them successful. One company interviewed as part of this study began using IPTs in 1992, even before they were a government requirement. They perceived the benefits as including a proper focus on products and enabling them to "get the products right the first time." Also, IPTs have allowed for greatly improved responsibility and accountability for technical performance measurements. Further, IPTs have eliminated in-house functional disputes and diminished internal strife.

The contact at this contractor did offer a caveat regarding the possibility of creating stovepipe IPTs that do not properly manage the process of integration. (This concern was also raised by more than one government official, who suggested the IPTs responsible for different parts of the aircraft could do more to integrate with other IPTs.) The contractor summed up its experience by saying that, while the organizational structure of IPTs is not cheaper and may in fact be more expensive than functional groups, recurring costs should be much lower. Unfortunately, with IPTs, as with many other decisions in the acquisition world, once a decision is made to take one path (for example, using IPTs), the costs of taking the alternative paths can only be estimated.

Cost Effects of IPTs

Two useful metrics to prove the value of IPTs are overall system life cycle cost and production cycle time. At the time this research was conducted, contractors could not offer specific cost savings from the use of IPTs in either category. They indicated that there were some up-front costs but that they expected to see significant savings in the long run.

At one plant, the general rule of thumb was that IPTs added 10 to 20 percent to the initial design costs. This could be the result of IPT participants from such disciplines as tooling, manufacturing, or logistics, who, under the historical model, would not have participated early in the design phase. Theoretically, with the emphasis on affordable, manufacturable designs, some of the traditional problem-solving during the fabrication and assembly of the first few aircraft should take place in the design IPTs, so the net overall system cost could be lower. Thus, IPT costs may be just a bookkeeping issue, with nonrecurring engineering costs reflecting some of what historically would have been accounted for in recurring manufacturing costs, especially for early production units. In addition, it could also be the result of a relatively new institutional mechanism that companies have less experience using efficiently. In short, IPTs represent a new practice that needs to be "learned." Over time, as companies gain experience dealing with the new organizational structures, the cost penalty of the IPT structure could diminish.

While contractors could not calculate overall savings from using IPTs, they did express confidence that these savings were real. There was some dissatisfaction with difficulties of coordinating the opinions of a diverse set of stakeholders and concern that the pendulum would swing back to functional stovepipes. Indeed, one person expressed the opinion that IPTs became stovepipes in their own right and could be poorly coordinated with the functional perspective and with lessons from other programs. Without careful management, IPTs, rather than being focused, multifunctional teams working to design a superior aircraft and resolve crosscutting issues, can become another version of ongoing committees, with the attendant bureaucratic costs and questionable output.

One of the first programs designed using IPTs, the F-22, has experienced some schedule and cost problems during the design phase, but these cannot necessarily be ascribed to the IPT structure itself. Rather, the challenges of the advanced technologies of the airplane, strict customer requirements, funding challenges, congressional attention, and other effects outside of the contractor's control affected the development cycle time of the aircraft. However, a strong measure of the success of the IPTs will be whether the design can be manufactured for less than traditional cost models would forecast. Only time will tell on this issue, after more aircraft are produced. (Note that as of the time of this writing, no production configuration F-22s had been manufactured.)

COMPUTER-AIDED DESIGN TECHNOLOGY

The second major innovation that has radically altered the product design process in the aircraft industry is that made possible by CAD[2] technology. CAD exemplifies a new technology that is not driven by lean manufacturing concepts but when used properly can enhance the lean production system. It enables up-front attention to quality, manufacturability, and cost. Data created in the design phase can be used to drive manufacturing, to connect to suppliers, and to give workers instructions and insight into what they should be doing.

Early aircraft were designed by engineers drawing on paper with pencils, T squares, and French curves. Analyses of such design issues as strength calculations were done with slide rules, then with mainframe computers. While many excellent aircraft were designed using these tools, managing and integrating the hundreds of paper drawings and schematics was an incredibly difficult task. A mistake on one drawing could impact the structure of the entire airplane. No efficient way existed to test whether all the parts would fit together properly in advance. Time-consuming and expensive mockups were built to help determine whether parts would fit together.[3] Factory floor workers became skilled at using shims and other makeshift solutions to compensate for ill-fitting pieces. Using the process of engineering change orders (ECOs), design engineers reworked these and other design flaws throughout the production life of the aircraft. The traditional learning curves in aircraft production were in part a function of the process of figuring out how to manufacture aircraft that did not fit together as originally designed. In some cases, pro-

---

[2]Popular CAD programs include CATIA, UNIGRAPHICS, and composite-specific Verisurf and Fibersim.

[3]Engineers at one aircraft plant described how as soon as individual components, especially those involving wiring and tubing, were completed, they were rushed to the mockup and installed to stake a claim for optimal space.

duction workers actually learned that they had to manufacture or assemble parts of aircraft differently from the specified designs.

The first digital design innovation was two-dimensional (2-D) drawing tools, which reduced the need for time-consuming repetitive drafting of redesigns. Computer tools enabled the 2-D designs to be easily iterated and changed, allowing for somewhat more experimentation in design. But integrating all the drawings to examine manufacturability still was exceedingly difficult.

The next innovation, three-dimensional (3-D) wireframe technology, modeled the outline of parts and allowed some initial testing of manufacturing fit. With 3-D wireframe design tools, designers could expand their concepts into three dimensions more easily. Changes made to one part during the design process automatically flowed through to all the other parts that the change affected. Finally, the current best practice design technology, 3-D solids modeling, allows the design engineer to develop a complete digital dimensional representation of the final part and offers very strong software programs that determine if the parts can be assembled without problems, including gaps requiring shims or part overlaps. Current modeling technology also allows 3-D design and manufacturing of tools on which the parts will be made and virtual simulations to determine whether workers will be able to fabricate and assemble complex parts. Figure 4.1 offers a 3-D example of some structures of the F-22.

Another benefit of 3-D solid design is that related CAD programs and other digital technology allow manufacturers to enter the data developed during the design process into a shared digital database and use it throughout the production of the airplane. For example, electronic work instructions for factory floor workers can be developed using this data. Factory floor workers can access the task requirements using terminals located near their workstations, cutting the need for printed instructions and allowing them a three dimensional view of the part. The flexibility of digital technology means that changes can be easily and immediately communicated to these workers. Design data can also be processed through a translator program that produces code for computer numerically controlled (CNC) machine tools used in part fabrication, thus saving the costs of manual programming. In composite part manufacturing, the pro-

RAND*MR1325-4.1*

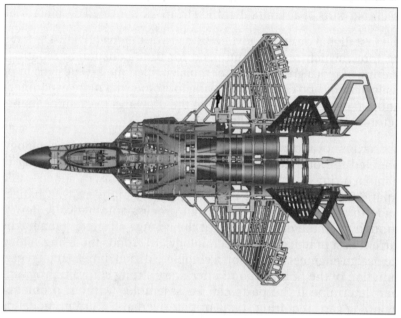

SOURCE: Lockheed Martin.

Figure 4.1—F-22 3-D Design

gramming of optical laser ply alignment tools used in the laying up of composite plies can be developed from the same design database, again reducing programming costs.

The design data can also be used by the purchasing and supplier management function, especially if an integrated Enterprise Resource Planning (ERP) tool is in use at the facility. The electronic data can be used to develop a list of what needs to be purchased from suppliers. Suppliers of parts can gain access to the design schematics to program their own CNC machines. (Of course, in a truly lean environment they will have been involved in the design of the relevant parts during the development phase.)

CAD technology is universally used at contractors, who all reported good experiences with it. They offered many anecdotal examples of improvements. However, engineers did not universally support the argument that the new digital technology allows for substantial reductions in the cycle time or engineering hours for design. Rather, designers seem to use these more powerful design tools to produce better designs in the same amount of time, rather than the same designs in less time. The tools, however, have allowed for increased design iterations. The DoD Planning, Programming, and Budgeting System (PPBS) schedule was often mentioned by companies as having a greater impact on cycle time during design than the actual development work activities. This represented the design engineers' perspective on the advantages of CAD. Savings at a program level may be significant from an integration perspective as well as from the other efficiencies from the common 3-D database discussed here. In addition, as experience with 3-D systems increases and the workload of design/development activities becomes more refined, time allocated to design engineers may be reduced.

A considerable amount of information is available from the contractors on the many benefits of CAD, and some data support it. One company used digital definition of the manufacturing process on a recent program and saw a substantial reduction in the number of ECOs versus a similar product designed 20 years ago. Twenty months after the start of the older program, manufacturing difficulties had driven 6,500 engineering changes. By contrast, 20 months after the start of the new program, only 900 engineering changes had been required, a number much lower than the forecast 3,200. The company gave credit for the drop in ECOs to both digital process definition and IPTs.

One company offered a telling example of how improvements in the design process are actually decreasing assembly costs. On one program, the first aircraft took less than 40 percent of the budgeted assembly labor hours. The static test article was then assembled in about half that time, or about 20 percent of the time originally budgeted. Another 10 percent reduction in actual assembly hours was experienced for the second full-up aircraft assembly, or less than 20 percent of the budgeted time.

Another company estimated that design-to-build information release time would decrease 60 percent using these tools.

In another example, seen in Table 4.1a, one company offered a less-clear example of the benefits of digital design. (These numbers have been altered proportionally to hide the identities of the programs.)

At first glance, the information presented by the contractor showed a benefit in 3-D solids design. When the hours were normalized for weight to come up with engineering hours per pound, a common metric of efficiency, the results are less clear, as shown in Table 4.1b.

Both 3-D technologies offer vast improvements over 2-D drawings. On an hours-per-pound basis, however, the advantage of the 3-D

Table 4.1a

Effect of Different Design Technologies on Nonrecurring Labor Hours of a Specific Subassembly

	Platform		
Activity	A 2-D Drawings	B 3-D Wireframe	C 3-D Solids
Design	32,347	31,071	14,975
Strength	21,802	21,663	19,005
Tool Design	33,254	15,488	9,756
Manufacturing Engineering	NA	9,655	7,226
Tool Fabrication	78,490	94,097	49,038
Total	165,893	171,973	100,000
Weight Factor (pounds)	281.10	564.25	254.50

Table 4.1b

Effect of Different Design Technologies on Nonrecurring Labor Hours Per Pound of a Specific Subassembly

	Platform		
Activity	A 2-D Drawings	B 3-D Wireframe	C 3-D Solids
Design	115.1	55.1	58.8
Strength	77.6	38.4	74.7
Tool Design	118.3	27.4	38.3
Manufacturing Engineering	NA	17.1	28.4
Tool Fabrication	279.2	166.8	192.7

solids design over 3-D wireframe design is much less obvious. One explanation may be that Platform B represented an evolutionary design, so design hours would be expected to be lower because the platform was not entirely new. On the other hand, Platform A represents a relatively complex aircraft with relatively large amounts of advanced materials. Hours per pound for 2-D drawings could conceivably be lower if Platform A had been a simpler structure, meaning that the advantage of the 3-D methods may be overstated above. Another issue may be that design time is not strictly a linear function with weight; it takes relatively fewer hours per pound to build larger structures than smaller ones. This means that the advantage of 3-D wireframe techniques are overstated above because the hours per pound on a smaller platform should be larger.

A final explanation is supported by interviews with engineers at the research sites. Cutting cycle time is difficult when government budget requirements drive development schedules. The engineers suggested that advanced design tools were often used to make aircraft designs better in that given amount of time (through more iterations) rather than design to a reduced cycle time. It should be noted that every person interviewed as part of this study indicated that 3-D solid techniques were a dramatic improvement over older methods.

This one example illustrates the difficulty in obtaining defensible cost data to prove the point that new technologies reduce costs. Any new technologies may require some learning before they result in cost savings. There have not been enough units produced using 3-D solids design technology to support claims of a long-term reduction in manufacturing costs, although initial data do support this. What this example suggests is that if contractors and customers are truly concerned about cost, attention must be paid to how new tools are implemented. Again, as experience with 3-D solids modeling tools increases, it may become clearer exactly where the savings are, and time and dollars estimated for design activities may be reduced.

OTHER LEAN ENABLERS—DESIGN PHILOSOPHIES THAT REDUCE MANUFACTURING COSTS

Attention to manufacturability in the design phase drives certain approaches by design engineers. Again, conscious up-front attention paid to costs, quality, and cycle time shape the design in a number of ways. To ease assembly, for example, parts are unitized wherever possible and cost-effective. Part standardization offers the possibility of volume discounts and other benefits.

Unitization/Part Count Reduction

Lean manufacturing relies on the continuous search for ways to reduce effort and increase product quality and incorporates into its philosophy any tools and concepts that assist in that goal. One of these tools is part count reduction. Womack et al. (1990) state that the front bumper of a GM Pontiac Grand Prix had 10 times as many parts as a Ford Taurus front bumper. This means GM had more parts to manage during design, more inventory numbers to manage, possibly a greater number of suppliers, more fasteners, more parts to fit together, and so forth. In short, simpler designs with fewer parts are easier and less expensive to build and less likely to have quality problems. This involves fabricating larger parts and then building up subassemblies from these larger parts. Changing designs so that larger parts are fabricated instead of being built up from smaller parts is known as *unitization*. As ever in lean manufacturing, attention to process quality is critical. Unitization means that individual parts represent a higher average cost and value. "Out of control" manufacturing processes that damage larger unitized parts are obviously more costly. One company provided an example of a redesign of a bulkhead using new technologies coupled with new design concepts and provided the two pictures in Figure 4.2 as illustrations.

Advanced metal processing, including high-speed machining[4] (HSM) and super plastic forming/diffusion bonding[5] (SPF/DB), makes unitization possible and enables a reduction in direct assembly labor hours. Companies often offered examples where high-speed machines replaced conventional machines as emblematic of lean manufacturing and the savings that it offered. The prime contractors described several examples of savings from unitization enabled by HSM.

---

[4]In HSM, cutter heads rotate at 25,000+ revolutions per minute.

[5]SPF/DB involves the fabrication of complex sheet metal components in a single forming and bonding operation using heat and pressure.

RAND*MR1325-4.2*

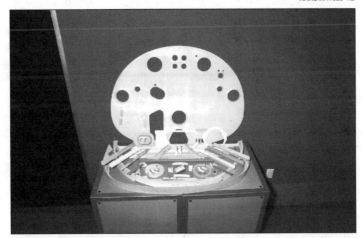

SOURCE: Lockheed Martin.

Built-up sheet metal bulkhead

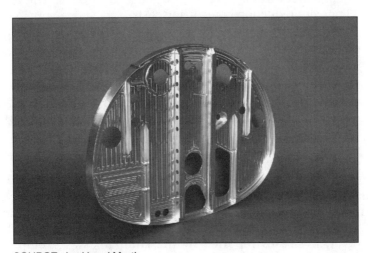

SOURCE: Lockheed Martin.

High-speed machined unitized bulkhead

Figure 4.2—Part Count Reduction/Unitization Example

- One company offered an example where a built-up part was replaced with one produced predominantly through HSM, leading to an overall 73 percent reduction in costs. Using Design for Manufacturing and Assembly (DFM/A) principles, the number of parts decreased from 44 to six. Pan stock items decreased from 445 to 108. Weight decreased from about 9.5 pounds to about 8.5 pounds. Assembly time decreased from 50 hours to 5.3 hours.

- Using HSM and unitization principles, another company reduced part count in a redesign by about one-third. In a different example, more than 700 part details and 10,000 fasteners were eliminated in an aft fuselage redesign, where the new part was produced with SPF/DB.

- A third company's design concept used HSM components with integral stiffeners and precise tongue-and-groove features for unitized, adhesively bonded assembles. In one case, a subassembly went from 19 detailed parts put together with 170 fasteners and weighing 2.7 pounds to one with three detailed parts put together with six fasteners weighing 1.9 pounds. This led to a 63 percent reduction in recurring costs.

- Another company did a trade study comparing an HSM unitized bulkhead with a conventionally built-up bulkhead. The unitized bulkhead took 39.5 hours to fabricate and assemble, instead of 115.3 hours for the conventional bulkhead. Part count was reduced from 100 to 56, the number of tools required was reduced from 95 to 19, fastener count declined dramatically from 483 to just over 40. Weight went from 16.5 to 13.8 pounds. Nonrecurring costs declined from approximately $1.285 million to $277,000, while recurring costs declined from $15,000 to $7,200.

Unitization offers a fine illustration of how incorporating the perspective of manufacturing engineers into the design process can cut the costs of direct manufacturing during the production phase. However, the cases reported by the companies as exemplifying potential savings from lean manufacturing offer a very limited perspective. Merely substituting high-performance machines for conventional machines may not be cost-effective in a larger sense because high-performance machine tools are considerably more expensive than conventional CNC machines. (The cost of these tools is captured in the tooling category if they are dedicated to the one program or product and in the factory overhead cost category if not and in either case should be considered in trade studies.) Furthermore, high-speed machining offers the potential for significantly reduced labor hours only if it is assumed that individual operators cannot oversee more than one machine at a time.[6] If they are able to operate multiple machines, they can use the run time of one conventional machine to perform set-up for another conventional machine. Information from managers at aircraft producers indicated that unionized workers in some locations have objected to the operation of multiple machines. Berggren (1992) indicates that even at Toyota, multimachine tending was made possible only after company-run "enterprise" unions replaced independent unions.

This discussion of efficiency is only one part of the HSM story. In unitization, HSM offers important benefits over conventional machining. In the HSM process, much less heat, which can negatively affect such important characteristics as material strength, is generated in the part being worked on. For technical reasons,[7] HSM allows aluminum to be milled to much thinner dimensions, so manufacturers can start from a large billet and machine out the desired part. In addition, with thinner webs and walls in parts made with HSM, part weight can often be reduced.

In short, new technologies can offer a mixed picture from the standpoint of lean manufacturing. While unitization can offer real savings and quality improvements, it may involve significant investments in tooling, which must be justified by sufficiently large volumes and reductions in direct labor hours to make the adoption of required technologies cost-effective.

Part Standardization

Another design contributor to lean manufacturing is through the standardization and reduction of types of parts on aircraft. An air-

---

[6]More than one company admitted that certain expensive new machines (not HSM machines) were not actually cost-effective. The machines were used as a signaling device to indicate that the companies kept abreast of the latest technology.

[7]One company listed the benefits of an Ingersoll advanced five-axis HSM mill as increased system stiffness, higher acceleration, active and passive damping, feed forward, and chatter recognition and control.

craft may have hundreds of different types of fasteners totaling in the hundreds of thousands. This translates to hundreds of inventory numbers, hundreds of part types to order, hundreds of bins of parts on the factory floor, and possibly dozens of suppliers. The large number of similar parts increases the potential for human error as assembly workers inadvertently use the wrong part.

Lean manufacturing aims to simplify production processes and reduce the potential for human errors, and one tool is the focus on limiting the number of different types of similar parts on the aircraft. Using only a few dozen instead of hundreds of kinds of fasteners can lead to cost savings in inventory and supplier management, may result in volume discounts, and can reduce the possibility of factory floor error. Design engineers who consciously attempt to limit the number of different types of similar parts contribute toward controlling costs.

One company performed a study of fasteners and found that often many different types were used just a few times on the aircraft. In the case studied, more than 50 percent of particular fasteners were used 20 times or fewer on the aircraft (with 44 percent of fastener types used 10 times or fewer). The contractor reported more than 135 combinations of tolerances and hole sizes, resulting in 12,000 distinct bins required to support production. Furthermore, specialized fasteners are often used instead of standard fasteners in aircraft production. These specialized fasteners can be extremely expensive. One company provided two examples where specialized fasteners on one program cost over 30 percent more than similar conventional aircraft fasteners.

SUMMARY RESULTS ON IMPLEMENTATION OF LEAN DESIGN AND DEVELOPMENT

Existing evidence on how lean production effects engineering design and development costs remains mixed. New design tools including 3-D solids modeling ease the design process and automate the necessary analytical work. However, initial evidence indicates that engineers are not necessarily using the tools to design aircraft more quickly with fewer overall engineering hours. Instead, they may be building a better aircraft using the same hours.

The defense aircraft design process is at the mercy of the government customer, so government schedule requirements are a driver of cost that the contractors cannot independently eliminate. As well, the process of making the transition in the design structures to IPTs has not been without its costs and difficulties. IPTs require a considerable amount of coordination across functions and between organizations. Companies face an organizational learning curve when they adopt new organizational structures, which might explain the circumstantial evidence that IPTs actually increase costs.

The most significant cost savings from developing aircraft according to lean principles should show up during the manufacture of the aircraft, not during the design process. Even in relatively small aircraft quantities (fewer than 500), the dollars spent on development are less than half of the production dollars. For large buys, this ratio may only be 10 percent. Further, the only two modern fighters using many of these lean principles (F-22 and F/A-18E/F) are still in the Engineering and Manufacturing Development (EMD) phase or very early production, so statistically relevant actual production benefits will not be evident for several years. The tools currently used to design the JSF are relatively new, and limited historical evidence exists to prove the overall savings from lean design. The proof will be whether the selected JSF prime contractor is able to produce that aircraft at the price that they are currently targeting.

Chapter Five

TOOLING

INTRODUCTION

Costs of tooling have their own distinct CCDR category. In this chapter, we describe the different aspects of tooling and some of the advances in tooling concepts relevant to lean production. Improvements in product design and tooling flexibility have the potential to lower costs and ease the manufacturing process. The CCDR definition for tooling can be found in Appendix C.

TOOLING IN THE CCDR

The tooling CCDR cost category is divided into two groups, design and fabrication. Tooling also has recurring and nonrecurring aspects. Tooling in the CCDR sense refers to the special tools and equipment unique to a particular weapons system. General-purpose tooling (cranes, autoclaves) usable for different products is normally accounted for in the factory overhead category. Nonrecurring tooling refers to the initial tool design and in-house fabrication or purchases, as well as subsequent buys for replacement or to increase manufacturing rates. Recurring tooling captures costs for maintenance and repair of tooling unique to manufacturing a particular weapon system as well as wear parts, such as drill bits.

Note that lean principles hold engineering and tooling to be intrinsically related. Designing for lean manufacturing involves careful attention to minimizing all tooling costs. For example, parts that self-locate minimize the need for jigs and other tools that hold parts in the proper position for assembly. Flexible tooling that can be used for more than one part decreases the overall investment in tools.

Organizing manufacturing lines according to lean principles should enable output to be increased in any given line, thereby reducing the costs of procuring additional tooling. The same techniques and design concepts, coupled with attention to costs, that reduce assembly hours can also be applied to reduce tooling costs.

ADVANCES IN TOOLING

Self-Locating Parts

One mechanism to reduce tooling is to design and fabricate parts with devices that properly align them in the next higher assembly or to adjoining parts. For example, small tabs or tongue-and-groove features in adjoining parts can help locate them in the proper position during final joining, whether using fasteners, adhesives, or some other assembly method. This can dramatically reduce the number of dedicated assembly tools required to hold different parts and subassemblies in place as they are joined.

Flexible Tooling

Another technological advance that contributes to lean is flexible tooling. Flexible tools can be used in the fabrication or assembly of multiple parts rather than being dedicated to a particular part or a small family of parts. Ideally, they should also have very low setup times. Tools that can make many different parts can be used to fill in and reduce bottlenecks by allowing for the manufacturing of whatever subassemblies are needed to continue the flow of aircraft through the plant. They can also help reduce total investment in nonrecurring tooling, because fewer tools dedicated to particular parts are needed. For example, "pogo beds" are holding devices consisting of a grid of small rods with suction devices at the end. The rods can be individually raised and lowered so that parts of different shapes can be placed on the beds that have been programmed to match the shape of a part or subassembly. The vacuum applied by each suction device holds the parts tightly in place during processing by machine tools.

Another classic example of flexible tooling is offered by optical laser ply alignment of composites. Rather than using hard templates in the shape of each ply to mark out where to locate the actual ply on the lay-up tool, laser ply alignment involves an outline of laser light projected onto the tool to guide the mechanics in placing each ply of composite material onto the previous plies. Benefits include lower labor hours, elimination of the design and purchase or manufacture of templates, faster fabrication (ply laying), and elimination of storage space and maintenance of the templates. Costs include the purchase and programming of the laser. (The costs of programming the laser are not significant if a translator program is used with the digital data from the design database.) One company estimated that overall, laser ply alignment systems save as much as 67 percent in nonrecurring tooling costs. In one case, hard template tooling took an average of 70 hours to fabricate. The N/C programming required for laser ply alignment took only 22 hours.

Other New Tooling Technologies

Other new technologies improve productivity and quality and reduce cost. For example, high-speed machine tools offer many contributions to leanness. One company listed the following benefits: design optimization/learning, span time reductions, reduced assembly requirements, improved part finishes and tolerances, ability to accommodate all part families and unitized structures, producibility for high angularity parts, and burr reduction.

These new technologies may or may not be used in a lean way—e.g., to improve flow of the value through the plant. A new high-speed machine tool located in a traditional machine shop will certainly process batches more quickly. In this capacity it contributes to a reduction of overall value-added cycle time, but the overall part or product cycle time may not be decreased measurably if the part is fabricated and then is placed in a holding area awaiting the next operation. However, high-speed machines can contribute to lean production in many other ways by taking advantage of their capabilities in the design process to develop unitized structures.

SUMMARY DISCUSSION OF LEAN TOOLING

Several of the companies participating in this study provided interesting examples of how they planned to reduce the tooling required on future programs. These included both design features (e.g., self-locating parts) and new tooling technologies and concepts. In one case, analyzing product flow through the plant led to an estimate that rate tooling could be reduced by one full assembly line. Lean implementation does have a potentially significant effect on tooling costs in the manufacture of military aircraft, but there is as yet little actual data from full-rate production in a lean environment.

Chapter Six

MANUFACTURING

INTRODUCTION

In this chapter, we describe in somewhat more depth the complexities of how lean production affects the manufacturing function. We look at both major process changes and enabling tools. We provide specific examples of lean implementation efforts and the savings that resulted. The companies that participated in this study demonstrated many lean pilot projects where savings were achieved in manufacturing functions. In terms of aircraft recurring labor costs at the prime contractor level, manufacturing constitutes more than half of the direct labor hours, so it is a very important area for focusing lean manufacturing techniques. The CCDR definition for manufacturing is in Appendix C.

At the most basic level, lean manufacturing is about making better products more quickly and at lower cost with minimum waste, which places a great deal of focus on production operations in the factory. A lean factory is one where machines are arranged in an orderly fashion to enable rapid and efficient product movement. It is a factory with minimal work-in-process and finished goods inventories, where products are built only when customer orders are received. It is a factory where workers pay attention to the quality of the product they are building and can perform inspections and simple machine maintenance. A lean factory is clean and orderly, without dirt or untidiness that can harm the product and without potential dangers that can harm workers.

Lean manufacturing operates on two levels on the factory floor. First, lean incorporates such large-scale philosophies as producing goods according to customer demand (pull production), arranging tools so parts flow smoothly and efficiently through the production stream (cellular manufacturing, producibility), and changing tools quickly to produce different parts (flexibility). Second, lean manufacturing is about incorporating a wide variety of specific best practices. These range from the kitting of parts and tools to such simple improvements as shadowboxes to store tools to the 6S philosophy about keeping the factory clean and safe to digital technologies aiding manufacturing, such as electronic work instructions.

LEAN MANUFACTURING IN THE FACTORY

Lean manufacturing focuses on cutting costs and waste, but it goes well beyond Taylor's "scientific management" attention to how the specific tasks are performed. Instead, lean manufacturing pays attention to two different aspects of the production process, the value-added steps, which include all work that contributes directly and positively to the manufacture of the product, and the non-value-added work, which includes everything else done to the product and in the plant. Machining time, when the product is actively being formed, shaped, or otherwise manipulated to bring it into conformance with the final design, is value-added work. Many sources of non-value-added work exist, including rework of a part or sub-assembly resulting from out-of-control processes. All non-value-added work can be classified as waste.

Much previous work on efficiency improvements and cost reduction in the factory has focused on the value-added portion of the work. For example, making production processes more efficient through investments in new machine tools has been an ongoing effort. Reducing the non-value-added portion of processes received less attention before the lean manufacturing. A notional example, as seen in Figure 6.1, reveals why the focus on the total value stream offers powerful insights.

In the base case, 20 percent of any particular effort might be related to value-added effort and 80 percent non-value-added. One common example is cycle time. In this case, 20 percent of the time the part is in the factory it is actually being worked on, and 80 percent of the time it is either in beginning inventory, awaiting a process,

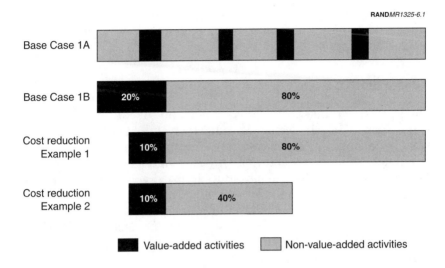

RAND*MR1325-6.1*

Figure 6.1—Effects of Reductions in Value-Added and
Non-Value-Added Work

awaiting transport to another tool, being moved to another tool, or in final inventory, awaiting installation or delivery to the customer. Base case 1A graphically demonstrates how periods of activity are interspersed with significant amounts of time that the part is spent in queue or traveling. The second depiction of the same base case (1B) totals the value-added and non-value-added portions of the time to arrive at 20 percent and 80 percent. (Note that 80 percent is actually a very low proportion for non-value-added cycle time in most non-lean factories—more than 95 percent was often mentioned as the non-value-added cycle time in a factory.) In the first cost reduction example, efforts focused on the value-added portion of the process have yielded a formidable 50 percent reduction in value-added production time that results in a cycle time of 90 percent of the base case. Lean manufacturing advocates attention to the non-value-added portion as well, as in the second cost-reduction example. Here, a 50 percent reduction in both contributors to overall cycle time results in a cycle time that is one-half its original figure, with 80 percent of the savings achieved through the reduction in non-value-added activities. Of course, in terms of costs, the value-added time (for example, on-machine time) may be much more expensive than the non-value-added time, so analyses must evaluate all aspects of the flow time/cost processes to develop optimal lean manufacturing production flows.

PULL PRODUCTION

Ideally, the manufacturing process does not begin until an order from a customer has been received, which should send a signal to start production. Rather than building to some set production schedule, in lean manufacturing, orders from the customer start the production process. This helps reduce finished-goods inventories, as each item produced has a customer already. Producing to customer demand also reduces waste as unwanted output does not sit in finished-goods inventory, perhaps getting damaged or becoming obsolete. But producing to customer demand requires that lean companies develop flexible production processes to respond to the specific demands of each customer, to quickly produce the desired configuration. The length of time to produce a finished good, or cycle time, needs to be minimized so that specific customer demand can be met quickly and efficiently. This involves a drastic change of mindset for many companies that build according to a schedule that optimizes machine use, producing inventory that then must be aggressively marketed to customers, sometimes at discounted prices to move the products.

This lean ideal denotes a significant departure from historical manufacturing planning. Rather than producing directly to orders, managers traditionally would predict demand for their product and plan their production to match this prediction. If they guessed wrong, either expensive finished goods inventory would stack up waiting to be sold or profit opportunities would be missed as customers wanted more output of a different type than the factory could produce. Producing to customer demand eliminates these problems but requires a different production philosophy combined with very efficient processes to meet customer needs in a timely manner.

Pull production is to a large extent built into the aircraft production mindset. Both commercial and military aircraft production are geared toward specific orders from customers. Prime military contractors build planes that have been actually committed to by the customer, to an agreed-on schedule instead of speculatively. Aircraft manufacturers are in an excellent position, therefore, to work backward from known delivery dates to schedule production. Cycle time reduction can still be an important area of cost saving and improved customer service. Properly applied techniques from lean manufacturing can reduce this cycle time and help keep costs down. Taking a longer time to build an aircraft means that both costs and the risk of quality problems increase as the aircraft accumulates costs based on its status as part of Work in Progress (WIP) inventory, without operational availability to the customer/operator.

CELLULAR PRODUCTION AND SINGLE-PIECE MANUFACTURING FLOW

A lean factory looks very different from a factory engaged in batch production in a number of ways. An experienced eye might first notice the different arrangements of the machine tools, which reflects a number of related lean principles and best practices such as pull production and inventory reduction.

Traditionally, manufacturing plants were organized into what can be called departments based on the type of processing that was being done. For example, basic metal machining done on similar tools would be in one department. All the related machine tools, such as grinders or cutters or drilling machines, would be located in the grinding or cutting or drilling department. Parts and assemblies would move from area to area depending on what needed to be done to them next. Any particular part could move back and forth into and out of one department several times. A considerable amount of movement was involved, as well as waiting time for parts to be picked up and moved around. Since it is costly to move parts individually, usually some batch of a number of parts would be worked on and finished and the entire batch would be moved at one time.

In the ideal lean manufacturing plant, tools are arranged in cells by product. The focus within the cell is not on the function or on the particular process but on the part or product. All the machines that work on a particular part are in sequence so that as soon as one process is finished, the part can be moved to the next operation. Keeping the product moving reduces the amount of inventory stacked up waiting to be worked on. Also, a quality problem caused by one process becomes quickly obvious in the next process. (Under traditional batch manufacturing, a process that causes a quality problem perhaps because of an out-of-tolerance machine may not be discovered until the entire batch is finished and moved to the next department.)

A simple example demonstrates the benefit from the reduction of batch sizes (see Table 6.1). In this example, each part must go through four processes before it is completed. Processing one part by any process takes one unit of time. The columns labeled T_1 through T_{10} represent the 10 units of time in the process, with contents of that cell representing what has been worked on in that time period. (The moment in time represented is actually the end of the time period, T_n.) S1 through S4 refer to the different machine stations or processes that create the finished product.

In the first case, the batch size is three. Each batch is represented here with a different letter, so that its progress can be tracked through the "factory." As parts are worked on at a particular station, they move from the left side of the cell to the right side of the cell, signifying a move from inventory waiting to be worked on to inventory that has been processed and is waiting for the completion of the whole batch so it can be moved to the next station. Finished items are expressed in upper-case letters to symbolize the higher value of these items that have been processed. The group of parts does not move to the next station until all three parts in the batch are complete.

In the first example, there is one unit of finished inventory at the end of ten units of time. A customer must wait ten units of time to receive a single unit of the product that it has ordered. Eleven parts make up the WIP inventory. A processing or quality problem caused at the first station (S1) would not be discovered until the first batch of parts moves to the second station during the fourth time period (T_4), possibly resulting in four scrapped parts before the out-of-tolerance situation was discovered and corrected. If quality inspection occurs at the very end of the production process, as many as 13 parts would be scrapped or reworked, depending on what process was causing the problem. (If it was the first process, the three parts that had moved to final inspection; the nine parts that were undergoing pro-

Table 6.1

Case 1:   Batch Production

Station	T_1	T_2	T_3	T_4	T_5	T_6	T_7	T_8	T_9	T_{10}
S1	aa A	a AA	AAA	bb B	b BB	BBB	cc C	c CC	CCC	dd D
S2				aa A	a AA	AAA	bb B	b BB	BBB	cc C
S3							aa A	a AA	AAA	bb B
S4										aa A
WIP	3 parts	3 parts	3 parts	6 parts	6 parts	6 parts	9 parts	9 parts	9 parts	11 parts
Finished parts										A

NOTE: Each numbered T designation represents the end of a given time period. Lower-case units on the left side of each cell are waiting to be worked on. Upper-case on the right side of the cell indicates parts that have been processed and are waiting to be moved to the next function. Upper-case units finishing the final process (S4) have completed all four stations and are finished products.

cesses two, three, and four; and the unit being worked on in station one while the problem was discovered would all have to be fixed.)

In the second case (see Table 6.2) the batch size is one. As each part is finished, it is moved immediately to the next machine where processing begins. (Note that the inventory waiting to be worked on, represented as lower-case letters at the left side of the cells in Table 6.1, does not exist in this second example.)

In the second table, there are seven finished parts at the end of 10 units of time. A customer only has to wait four units of time until the first part is ready for delivery. There are only three parts in WIP inventory at the end of time 10, and no more than four parts in inventory at any given time. Parts are never in queue awaiting work but are undergoing nearly constant processing.

It should be noted that, over a longer period of time, the number of finished parts in the first process approaches those in the second example. At the end of 100 units of time, single piece flow production would result in 97 parts. The three-piece batch process would result in 91 parts. However, the one-piece flow example does have the advantage that quality and machine problems are discovered more quickly. A processing problem at the first station (S1), whether caused by a machine that is out of tolerance or by error from an insufficiently trained operator, would be discovered quickly, during the second time period (T_2), after the part moved to the second station (S2). Remedial action could quickly fix the offending problem before many parts that had to be scrapped or reworked were made. Even if all quality assurance activities took place at the end of the production process, after the parts are in station four (S4), there still would only be four parts that need to be scrapped or reworked. This is a sharp contrast to the batch manufacturing example, where first station problems would be discovered at the second station, after three bad parts have been built, or perhaps in quality assurance after production is complete, when at least 12 parts would need to be scrapped or reworked.

Single-piece flow production is intrinsically related to cellular production, with machines in successive operations close to each other with related cells abutting one another. Parts move quickly between

Table 6.2

Case 2:   Single-Piece Flow Production

Station	T_1	T_2	T_3	T_4	T_5	T_6	T_7	T_8	T_9	T_{10}
S1	A	A	A	B	B	B	C	C	C	D
S2		A	A	A	B	B	B	C	C	C
S3			A	A	A	B	B	B	C	C
S4				A	A	A	B	B	B	C
WIP	1 part	2 parts	3 parts	3 parts	3 parts	3 parts	3 parts	3 parts	3 parts	3 parts
Finished parts					A	AA	AAA	AAA B	AAA BB	AAA BBB

NOTE: Each numbered T designation represents the end of a given time period. Units finishing the fourth process (S4) are complete.

stations, eliminating the non-value-added work of transportation and reducing cycle time. Parts are processed individually and then easily moved a foot or two to the next operation.

Alternatively, under the "traditional" model, where the processes occur in distinct departments, it makes more sense to produce parts in a larger batch rather than singly, to spread the costs of transportation to the next process across more than one part. However, moving the parts also adds to cycle time to produce the part and increases WIP inventory, which may be further increased if no one is available immediately to move the product. During this delay, the product might be harmed by environmental contaminants, physical damage, or even obsolescence. The delay might also increase the costs of quality, as has already been discussed, when problems created by one machine are not discovered until the entire batch gets to the next station instead of after a single part moves on. Batch production deals with quality problems by maintaining an inventory of parts that have undergone the first process and would allow the second machine to keep working even if defective parts are found or if parts are damaged in transit. Inventory provides a buffer in batch manufacturing, although a buffer with significant costs. The batch method also increases required floor space to store the excess inventory and any extra machines required to maintain production levels, given inefficient processing.

Note that batch manufacturing should not necessarily be considered an example of poor management. If lean manufacturing principles have not been incorporated in the rest of the plant, batch production offers distinct benefits. For example, if the parts produced at the plant are widely varied, there might be significant setup times to reconfigure the machines for different types of parts. Producing similar parts in large groups is seen as being one way to increase machine utilization rates. Without pull production, parts may be produced for inventory rather than for particular customers. Also, if one machine broke and required repair, the next machines in the process would not necessarily lie idle if they were working with batch inventory. However, the goal of lean manufacturing is to make parts efficiently in batch sizes of one to avoid having to maintain these buffers. If lean manufacturing techniques are prevalent throughout, the costs inherent in batch production can be avoided.

Lean/best practice manufacturing does not assume that lengthy setup times or temperamental machines prone to breakdowns are normal aspects of production. Rather, it looks at these as issues that can be solved through careful analysis. Manufacturing engineers and skilled, trained operators can engage in short-term or long-term projects to deal with these issues. Lean manufacturing also consciously considers ways of reducing non-value-added stages as well as making value-added steps more efficient. This has driven the attention to reducing cycle time and transportation to eliminate costs.

Cellular production involves intense analytic study of the factory floor to enhance flow of the product through the factory. Machines should be located so that each product can move smoothly, and for the shortest distance, during processing. (Machines are often arranged so that the manufacturing cell has a U shape, to minimize part and people travel.) Improving flow also helps cut cycle time of manufacturing, and work in process inventory, with its attendant costs. Also, the number of operators may be reduced; fewer people are needed to move large batches of product from one machine to another.

Moving to a cellular lean production framework often involves the creation of pictures mapping out part or person travel. These are occasionally referred to as spaghetti charts, as traditional movements often resemble a big bowl of pasta, with the strands representing the travel path of the part or person. In contrast, a plant laid out to minimize part movement has a much simpler chart (see Figure 6.2.)

Note that the benefits of cellular production are limited unless the entire manufacturing floor is reorganized into cells. Unless all cells in the plant are lean, or the lean cells are on the critical path through the factory, parts may speed through some areas and sit around in other areas waiting to be worked on. Some WIP inventory will be reduced resulting in cost savings, but these savings may be small without a consistent plantwide effort to cut inventory.

In fact, lean manufacturing specifically examines this possibility as it calls for a continual analysis of bottlenecks, areas where inventory is building up because of poorly organized processes or insufficient

RAND*MR1325-6.2*

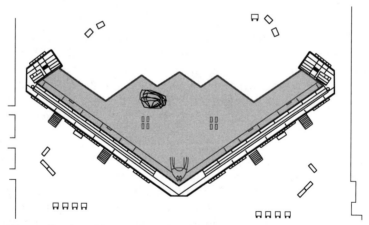

Preparation time–3 hours. Walk pattern–26+ trips. Process time–8.4 hours.
SOURCE: Northrop Grumman.

Before lean event

Preparation time–0 hours. Walk pattern–0 trips. Process time–1.62 hours.
SOURCE: Northrop Grumman.

After lean event

Figure 6.2—Before (Nonlean) and After (Lean) Process Flows

machine capacity. Focused remedial actions called *kaizen* events can be used to study and (ideally) quickly correct problem areas. Because lean manufacturing looks for a continual improvement[1] of flow through the plant, and as each bottleneck is removed and production is speeded up, by definition a new spot can be improved.

In production organized in assembly lines, such as in car manufacturing, this means that the pace of production is continually increased. Bottlenecks are identified at areas where workers can no longer keep up the pace. If they cannot perform the required functions, they can stop the assembly line until the bottleneck is resolved. By speeding up the line, assembly line production offers an efficient way of identifying areas that increase overall cycle time. This technique is less applicable in aircraft manufacturing, where low production volumes combined with an extremely complex product mean that assembly lines are not used.

TAKT TIME

Takt time describes how frequently final outputs should be produced in order to satisfy demand. It is the ratio of how much time is available in a given period divided by how many parts or products are demanded by customers in that time. So if customers want two parts every day, and there is one eight-hour shift, the *takt* time is four hours. Under the lean manufacturing system, this number drives operations in the factory. The system is set up so that one final product is produced every four hours. All areas are organized so that the associated tasks can be performed in that amount of time, before the part moves to the next station. The work is "balanced" so that all workers are fully employed during the *takt* time period. If demand increases, *takt* time decreases, and the system is reorganized (perhaps workers are added) so that parts can be produced more quickly. The concept of *takt* time and line balancing are perhaps more obvious drivers of operations in high-volume factories where many items

---

[1]Lean manufacturing calls for attempts for continuous improvement in all areas, from initial design to final delivery. Every process and function should be the target of ongoing analysis and study to improve it, to make it more efficient, to reduce its costs. Hence, true implementation of lean manufacturing is not a one-time event but rather an ongoing process involving considerable commitment.

are produced in an hour on an assembly line than in aircraft factories where high volumes might mean 10 aircraft in a month with a *takt* time of two work days. Balancing activities so that all workers are fully employed for the two-day *takt* time is a very complex task, although it can be done. *Takt* time can also be used to plan production of subassemblies so that they are produced at the proper rate and can be assembled to produce aircraft at a steady pace.

Takt time can help planners identify tooling and manpower requirements. As orders for aircraft are generally known in advance, *takt* time can be used by manufacturing engineers for advance planning factory operations so that production operates efficiently. Ideally, the ratio helps planners balance different aspects of the production process so that they are produced in approximately the same time, enabling single-piece flow and reducing inventories.

VISUAL CONTROL

Visual control consists of many initiatives related to maintaining product flow. Production workers and others in the plant should be able to easily determine what is in queue to be worked on next. Operators working in the plant as well as managers walking through it should see a clean area without a lot of inventory, where SPC charts let everyone know where improvement efforts must be focused, where workers can tell at a glance if they have the proper tools and parts to do a job. Similarly, machine controls should be obvious so that mechanics and others can easily tell if they are running properly.

Housekeeping

One more prosaic contribution to the overall quality effort occurs as a function of keeping the factory clean. This contributes to better visual controls. With no unnecessary material in the way, production problems become more obvious, parts and tools can be located more quickly, and products are not at risk from foreign contaminants. In aircraft production, housekeeping is particularly important because of the risk of damage from FOD.[2] Keeping the plant clean also makes

---

[2]Foreign object debris or foreign object damage.

machine problems more obvious. If the floor under a machine is generally kept clean, oil leaks become immediately apparent.

Lean housekeeping is often referred to as the "Five Ss," which allude to five Japanese words regarding keeping cleanliness in the plant. Different translations have produced various "S" words like sort, sweep, simplify, straighten, shine, sustain, standardize, and self-discipline. Most U.S. facilities have implemented a "Six S" program, where the sixth S stands for safety.

Location of Tools/Shadowboxes

Another area where visual control applies is tool storage. Mechanics use a considerable variety of hand tools (as opposed to large fixed tools) in assembly operations. Traditionally, these may have been kept in personal toolboxes located where particular mechanics spent their time. If they wanted a particular tool, they searched through their toolbox to find the tool then brought it back to the stand. Company-owned tools might also be kept in a centralized tool crib (which may or may not be nearby) where mechanics had to go to and ask for the tool they needed. In a lean plant, however, tool cribs are near where tools are needed. This cuts wasted time and motion on the part of mechanics. Another technique is for tools used in a particular area to be stored together in "shadowboxes," which take several forms. Some companies draw outlines of particular tools on boards then put hooks to hang the tools on. The outlines function as a "shadow" of the tools, and it is instantly clear if any tool is missing or is stored in the wrong place. Mechanics know where the tools are without searching for them and know where to return the tools. A similar concept is to use foam inserts with cut-outs for each tool. In both concepts, groups of tools used on a single process can be stored together. When mechanics start working on a new part, they can pick up the entire tool set at once. Also, mechanics can move smaller shadowboxes to where they are working to reduce the trips they take for tools. Some companies purchase tools for particular tasks much as they package the parts together (see kitting, below) for the same assembly task. Thus, the worker has everything required to complete a specific task at the beginning of work.

Cost reductions from a rationalized system for tools[3] result from decreases in direct labor hours, cost of tool inventories, and reduced defects. With tools properly stored, tool inventories are easier to manage and extra tools can be eliminated or never purchased to begin with. Each mechanic becomes more efficient because the right tools are always available, perhaps allowing for reduced head count. Furthermore, there may be increased quality stemming from the proper tool being used for each task. Determining the exact amount that shadowbox concepts could save would require before and after studies of the amount of time mechanics spent searching for tools, determining excess tool inventories, and the cost of quality problems attributable to incorrect tools being used.

Shadowbox Kitting

A similar innovation is the preparation of packages of all the parts that the mechanic needs to complete an assembly task, called *kitting*. With properly prepared kits containing all the required parts laid out in shadowbox format, mechanics know immediately if all the parts are available before starting the assembly of a particular item. They can pick up (or have delivered) the entire set of parts needed at one time and bring them to the assembly location, reducing travel time spent locating parts. It reduces the likelihood of the wrong part or fastener being used. It would also reduce WIP inventory, as mechanics would not start on jobs that they could not complete until all the parts were available. Note that kitting also can help enable the pull manufacturing system, as empty kit boxes can be used as a physical replacement for *kanban* cards and sent to the beginning of the line to signal when production of a particular part should start. Figures 6.3a and 6.3b demonstrate typical part presentations before and after shadowbox kitting.

Cost reductions from shadowbox kitting result from the reduced time needed to locate parts by mechanics, which could lead to reduced head count. (Some increase in support labor must be acknowledged for those who prepare the kits for the mechanics on

---

[3]See preceding chapter on tooling.

RAND*MR1325-6.3a*

SOURCE: Lockheed Martin.

Parts presentation kit before lean

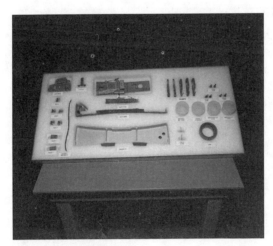

SOURCE: Lockheed Martin.

Parts presentation shadowbox after lean

Figure 6.3a—Before (Nonlean) and After (Lean) Shadowbox Kitting of Parts

the assembly line. Even if a one-for-one trade in direct labor hours for support labor took place, however, two reductions in cost occur. The first stems generally from lower support labor hour costs, and

RAND*MR1325-6.3b*

Tool presentation before kitting

 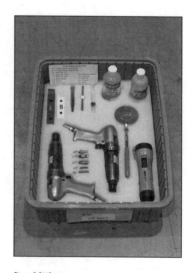

Tool presentation after kitting

SOURCE: Northrop Grumman.

Figure 6.3b—Before (Nonlean) and After (Lean) Kitting of Tools

the second is the reduced cycle time in the assembly process. (The kitting can be outsourced to take advantage of suppliers' generally lower labor rates.) Kitting can also result in reduced cycle time and lower WIP inventory. Part kitting helps rationalize the inventory system, perhaps making it obvious which parts are not currently being used in production so that they can be sold off and the space required for inventory can be reduced. Generalized savings estimates would vary by plant layout, complexity of the assembly, and even worker experience. However, savings could be determined by undertaking a before-and-after study of the time workers spent searching for parts (which could then be applied to additional assembly work, thereby reducing cycle time) and the savings related to reduced inventory.

MANUFACTURING BEST PRACTICES THAT ENABLE LEAN PRODUCTION

A considerable number of practices can help reduce costs and improve quality. As such, they can be incorporated into the lean manufacturing system as they reflect the lean philosophy of pushing for continuous improvement.

Total Productive Maintenance (TPM) offers workers job enrichment through greater responsibility in taking care of their machines. By doing regular maintenance tasks according to a predetermined schedule, the number of catastrophic machine breakdowns should be reduced. The advantage is that operators no longer must wait for dedicated maintenance personnel to perform these tasks, or they can perform the maintenance tasks during normally unproductive operator time. It may also give the workers a greater sense of ownership and pride in the machines and the processes. Ideally, the machines should have simple visual controls indicating how well they are working so that mechanics can be alert to problems earlier.

Electronic work instructions offer workers an information-rich reference to use during fabrication and assembly. Computer terminals placed near workstations can be accessed to provide lists of parts and tools that are needed, links to drawings and bills of materials, and specific step-by-step instructions on what to do. In some cases, step-by-step computer-generated pictures show the entire assembly sequence to the mechanic. Electronic work instructions are a particularly valuable tool during the complex production processes that characterize aircraft manufacturing. By contrast, in high-volume assembly line manufacturing, the work is broken down into small component steps that are performed repetitively by the same person. *Takt* time might drive balanced processes that take as little as a minute or two so one worker becomes quite expert at a specific task. Aircraft assembly volumes do not allow for such specialized division of labor, and processes tend to be more complex. Electronic work instructions are one tool to provide information to workers doing particular processes relatively rarely—perhaps once or twice a week in a high-volume aircraft line. Electronic work instructions can help workers figure out quickly how to proceed and help eliminate quality problems and associated waste from preventable mistakes. In addition, updated instructions reflecting incorporation of the latest engineering change orders/configurations can be provided immediately to the assembly line, thus preventing scrap or rework. In one company, electronic work instructions were expected to reduce total direct manufacturing labor by about 5 percent.

Markings on floor to position tools and equipment, or even places to bolt tools directly to the floor, reduce setup time in assembly and can improve fit as well as reduce waste from product defects.

In automobile plants, *Andon,* or ability of operators to stop the assembly line in case of problems, has been much touted. Aerospace has relatively low volumes and more complex operations performed over longer periods, so pulling a cord to stop the line is less applicable. However, mechanics should have the ability to stop production and alert management to problems. Recognizing the need for workers to provide feedback to engineers quickly, some companies have relocated engineers close to assembly areas and provided workers with "virtual hotlines" to contact the engineering/manufacturing staff rapidly when problems arise.

SUMMARY RESULTS ON IMPLEMENTATION OF LEAN MANUFACTURING

Visits to airframe manufacturers revealed a range of interesting projects, implementation strategies, and change philosophies. The prime contractors that participated in this study offered the results of a number of lean manufacturing projects. In many cases, these showed considerable savings in labor hours, in cycle times, and in floor space. All of the primes had at least initial experience with pilot projects on the factory floor, and some of this experience was quite extensive. These pilots are presented as they stood in the summer and fall of 1998. Since then, additional evidence may have been collected on these projects and additional projects.

It is useful to keep in mind the limitations of using pilot project savings for larger-scale implementation plans. One issue is how the projects were selected and whether they are representative of the entire manufacturing operation. They may have been ones where initial improvements were expected to come more easily (perhaps areas with chronic problems), the so-called "low-hanging fruit." Another is that smaller-scale changes may be easier to implement because less organizational or worker support is required. Scaling up lean techniques throughout the enterprise may require a considerable organizational effort. In addition, the "Hawthorne Effect" (Roethlisberger and Dickson, 1939; Mayo, 1945) may be operating during pilot programs as workers feel that management is paying attention to their analyses during *kaizen* events and hence increase their efforts. With these caveats in mind, what follows is a sample of larger lean visions, lean philosophies toward particular manufacturing areas, and results from some pilot projects.

Specific Examples of Savings from Lean Implementation

One company typical of those RAND visited was focusing its lean vision on a number of elements:

- Establishing a visual factory and pull system.
- Shortening cycle times and manufacturing spans.
- Focusing fabrication and assembly on value-added tasks.
- Standardizing support processes where practical.
- Reducing support labor costs.
- Reducing overall inventory investment.
- Providing timely, accurate data for decisionmaking.

Lean implementation has enabled some cycle time reductions at plants. For example, the span time of one product was reduced by 40 percent over four years. Credit was given to lean manufacturing initiatives as well as other efforts.

An example at another plant pointed out some of the contradictions in lean implementation. In one small extrusion processing cell, the number of employees was reduced from six to two after lean principles were instituted. The tremendous labor savings—66 percent—is not unique among efforts this small, but we found little evidence that such savings had been achieved in larger scale implementation efforts. It also points out one issue when implementing lean in the defense aerospace sector—the other four employees were surplused, by seniority. The firm indicated that the decision is "lean with fewer jobs or not lean with no jobs." Labor unions must share this philosophy if factories are to be made more efficient. While worker reductions may be required in the military aircraft sector, proponents of lean in the commercial world stress that cost reductions and quality improvements when implementing lean should result in greater volume of sales so workers may not have to be let go.

One company expected overall savings from lean manufacturing to be in the range of 10 to 15 percent savings. They stated that two-thirds of the effort in being lean or becoming lean occurs during development, with one-third occurring later on in production. However, 80 percent of the cost savings occur during production. The company claimed that using the new technologies without lean implementation would result in only 2 to 3 percent savings. Investments in lean programs were considered worthwhile because if the changes were implemented properly they would produce rapid paybacks.

Lean Transformation at Brownfield Plants[4]

Any new production philosophy is easier to implement at new facilities than at old, so-called "brownfield" plants, where large machinery is installed and manufacturing traditions are set. In any industry, when new contracts are awarded and new production plans are developed, the firms must decide whether to build new greenfield

---

[4]Brownfield plants are existing facilities, which may be less efficient than new plants (greenfields), which incorporate the latest technologies and process improvements.

plants or use existing ones, perhaps with modifications. New plants may be more expensive to build, but they can be designed to maximize the efficiencies from the most up-to-date production processes. One company took a second look at a planned new facility and was able to reduce the space required by two-thirds. Building a new line in a brownfield plant means that "monuments" built for some other program may have to be "worked around" for the new program.

This issue arises in the manufacture of composites because of the largest of the "monuments" used in the production of composites, autoclaves. Autoclaves are large chambers (shaped generally like cylinders, up to 40 feet in diameter) where high temperature and pressure can be applied to cure composite parts. In plants with existing autoclaves, production flow must be planned around these autoclaves to maximize flow, given that the curing process must occur at a particular place in the plant, unless significant investment is made in moving the autoclave. The necessity to cure parts in an autoclave can provide a constraint on lean product flow. A related issue is that monuments, such as autoclaves, are often built for large capacities so the largest parts can be cured inside them. To use them efficiently for smaller parts, large batches are cured at one time. (The operating expenses of autoclaves stemming from enormous energy requirements generally mean that parts that need to be cured build up until an autoclave-sized batch is developed.) However, the lean manufacturing philosophy is built on small lot sizes that flow quickly through the plant with minimal time spent in non-value-added activities, like queuing for the next process. Thus, regardless of a company's commitment to lean, physical monuments are always a constraint in brownfield situations.

Summary of Typical Savings

The following results summarize reports by military aircraft companies of savings from a sample of their efforts toward improving manufacturing processes:

- In a sample of 20 "leaned" cells and production areas, direct labor hours used to produce parts after lean principles were incorporated into production declined between 5 percent and 81 percent, with an average of 36 percent.

- Cycle time to produce parts was reduced between 13 percent and 93 percent (average 44 percent) (15 data points)

- Floor space savings ranged from 0 percent to 61 percent (average 24 percent) (12 data points)

- Part travel was reduced between 25 percent and 95 percent (average 61 percent) (10 data points)

- People travel was reduced between 23 percent and 94 percent (average 55 percent) (9 data points)

These averages should be considered suggestive rather than as offering a definitive result. Critically, the scales of different savings initiatives are unknown. Companies did not frequently offer information on the size of the effort, so it is difficult to know if a 50 percent reduction in labor meant the elimination of 1 job or of 20. The data suggest an inverse relationship between the size of the effort being leaned and the percentage savings, i.e., smaller pilots tended to yield much larger savings. Hence, analysts should use extreme caution when scaling up savings estimates from smaller pilots to the entire production process. In addition, savings in cycle time for noncritical path parts or subassemblies may not yield overall product cycle time reductions.

Because it is much more difficult to scale up lean production across cells than to lean out small production areas, it is impossible to assess the savings from lean manufacturing across the plant or enterprise by looking at these initial, suggestive results. Integrating lean across an entire factory floor presents many challenges that have not yet successfully been addressed in the aircraft industry. A more definitive assessment must wait for more complete data.

Furthermore, there exists the possibility of two kinds of selection bias in the reporting of these experiments. Companies may have selected their least efficient production areas to be leaned out first. This "low hanging fruit" would produce larger savings than the typical cell. Second, companies may have been biased toward describing their most successful efforts. There are no guarantees that the sample of lean areas they offered represented their most typical results. Unsuccessful efforts probably were not reported, not necessarily in any attempt to deceive or shade the results but because attention within companies is focused on efforts with positive outcomes, while projects that do not work are pushed aside and quickly become orphaned. Corporate focus on negative outcomes is productive when it captures lessons learned that can be used to make other efforts more successful, but this does not always take place.

That said, these results indicate that incorporating principles and tools of lean manufacturing has the potential to reduce costs in aircraft production. For reasons described above, applying any kind of a macro lean credit to a historically based CER cannot be analytically supported. Giving lean credit for the mathematical average of results of selected pilot cases reported by the companies is very likely too generous. A more conservative savings estimate of under 20 percent when lean principles are totally implemented throughout a plant is more reasonable but is not based on analytically derived evidence. However, whatever savings are experienced in the future will not come without significant effort and attention from company management and without a combination of incentives and pressure from the customer.

Chapter Seven

QUALITY CONTROL

INTRODUCTION

The focus on quality is one of the hallmarks of the lean production system. Quality is a major enabler of reduced costs, both directly through reductions in the quality assurance function and the cost of rework, and indirectly as it facilitates the reduction of inventory buffers. In this chapter, we discuss the critical role of quality in the lean system and report on efforts to improve quality at the companies that participated in this study. The full CCDR definition of quality control can be found in Appendix C.

FIRST-TIME QUALITY: A KEYSTONE OF LEAN

Quality assurance and manufacturing go hand in hand in lean manufacturing. First-time manufacture of quality products is one key to the efficiencies offered by lean production. This is not to say that traditional production did not consider quality important. Indeed, in any aircraft production, quality is *extremely* important. A quality problem that becomes evident while an airplane is in flight could have disastrous effects. Hence, a tremendous amount of time and effort is spent inspecting parts, subassemblies, and assemblies to make sure they were fabricated and built up properly. Those not meeting the rigid specifications are either scrapped or reworked to bring them into compliance. The catchphrase for this approach is that "quality is inspected in."

By contrast, in lean manufacturing, quality is "built-in." First-time quality receives tremendous emphasis, to avoid costly rework and scrapping of unsalvageable parts. Because poor production quality is a major source of costs and waste, lean manufacturing aims to eliminate these problems by building quality directly into the production processes rather than dealing with quality at the end. This requires a consistent focus on quality throughout the design and production process and when dealing with suppliers.

First-time quality is linked to other aspects of lean manufacturing also. Without first-time quality, single-piece flow with continuous smooth part movement becomes untenable. Without a focus on quality, WIP inventories are required to maintain production flow while quality problems are resolved. At the same time, single-piece flow allows instantaneous recognition of quality problems so they can be resolved before more than one part with the problem is built. Hence, the "inverse" of quality in the factory is inventory. Without first-time quality, inventory is required to keep machines running and to make sure that the parts are produced in a timely fashion for delivery to customers. Bad quality thus results in higher costs from rework and scrap and also because of the extra inventory needed to make sure downstream processes run smoothly. Inventory is an expensive buffer against mistakes, and the principles of lean manufacturing call for the removal of such costly buffers that conceal the extent and costs of the mistakes.

Companies can use a number of tools to enhance quality in the production process. These range from tools that measure quality and make sure processes are standardized to statistical tools that analyze processes and practices to processes on the factory floor.

A critical aspect of the lean quality philosophy is a focus on perfecting processes rather than on inspecting parts. Under the traditional manufacturing system, parts would be inspected and problem parts would be reworked or scrapped. Lean manufacturing aims to find the root cause of the problem and fix it. A part with a flaw is a signal that a larger problem needs to be taken care of. Root cause analyses offer formal processes (such as the "five whys"[1]) for discovering the causes of problems and addressing those.

---

[1]This technique refers to a process of asking questions to get at the real originating cause of a problem. For example, the question of why a part is not within tolerance should not merely be answered by saying the machine is out of tolerance. The machine may be out of tolerance because it has not been properly maintained,

Powerful tools can help determine which processes are problematic and need to be fixed. Statistical techniques, including statistical process control (SPC), can be used to determine if problem parts are idiosyncratic exceptions (which still need to be studied and remedied) or part of a larger problem based on the process. Operators can inspect the parts and provide the data for statistical analyses and in some cases can perform the analyses. Charts containing the results of these analyses are often posted near the relevant machines to help provide early indication of trends.

There are standards that companies can follow to help make sure their processes are consistent. For example, ISO-9000 certification is performed by an independent agency that documents whether processes are known and followed, ensuring control over different processes.

SPC tools and ISO-9000 certification can help companies reach the often-repeated quality goal of "Six Sigma." This refers to a normal distribution, with six sigma being six standard deviations from the mean, a very rare event. Six sigma quality translates to about 3.4 errors out of every million events. Essentially, to reach this demanding level of quality, each process has to be "error proofed"—that is, analyzed and reworked so that there is no room for a mistake in processing. Thus, process tolerances must be closely watched, in addition to having a design tolerance consistent with reasonable process tolerances.

Other practices, such as TPM, give workers a stake in how their machines are performing. Mechanics are trained to do simple machine maintenance and to monitor the performance of their machines on an ongoing basis. This should reduce quality problems caused by machines that are out of tolerance or break down because their care has been neglected.

---

because the responsible employees are overworked, because the operators do not have the authority to do simple maintenance, and so on and so on. When identified, the root cause can be fixed, which will prevent similar errors caused by that machine as well as errors caused by the same problem on other machines. The benefits of identifying and addressing the root cause of problems thus redound far beyond the original event.

REDUCTION IN COST OF QUALITY THROUGH LEAN PRACTICES

A number of promising policies were described at the participating companies. One company began a program of operator self-inspection in the early 1990s and has seen a resulting decrease in the number of factory quality control (QC) personnel. The project involved a systematic shift in responsibility for product quality from the traditional QC organization to the build teams and established "ownership" of product quality by those building the product. Low-risk QC inspections were eliminated and replaced with random inspections to make sure the self-verification processes were operating as planned. Critical inspections were maintained to safeguard the projects and the operators. The ratio of direct touch labor to QC labor increased from about 10:1 in 1992 to about 13:1 in 1998, representing an almost 25 percent net decrease in QC labor. With ownership in product quality, most business areas detect and report 98 to 99 percent of their own defects.

Another site offered a similar story of performance improvement, resulting in an expected 25 percent reduction of quality assurance (QA) personnel as a percentage of factory labor since 1992. This was the result of attempts to make quality a consideration at the beginning of the design process as well as formal programs to give production workers process ownership. They estimated that QA labor as a percentage of total factory labor declined from almost 23 percent in the early 1990s to about 19 percent in 1997, with an estimate of 17 percent in 1998.

Another company indicated that the trend in quality is for operator self-inspection, with QC people focused more on inspecting processes than inspecting individual parts. (This is something that the government had to agree to, however.) At that time, 11 percent of the touch labor at the company consisted of QC inspectors; their goal was to reduce QC to between 2 percent and 4 percent by using process auditing and worker self-inspection. A good audit plan was required to ensure quality is sustained. Workers had to be properly trained in inspection techniques, and acceptance by the union was required. To help win union support, QC workers (all of whom were experienced mechanics) would be guaranteed return rights to their former jobs as mechanics.

These initial forecast savings are encouraging and suggest that at least some defense aircraft manufacturers are paying attention to and trying to reduce the costs of quality. However, the costs of the QC function are often estimated and reported as some percentage of factory labor or manufacturing costs, rather than collected in their own right—most likely because of the difficulties of collecting dispersed information and applying it to specific work areas within a production area. (A subtle definition would incorporate the costs of direct QA personnel, the costs of scrapped parts leading to a worsening of the buy-to-fly material ratio, the costs of additional inventory buffers required when quality varies, and so forth.) As direct manufacturing labor is projected to be reduced through lean efforts, firms must decide whether the cost of QA will decline in proportion and keep the same estimating factor for the category or whether some other outcome is more likely. Full implementation of lean with attendant Six Sigma quality may mean that the cost of quality will decline at a greater rate than the costs of direct manufacturing. Although some companies have claimed this to be the case in their cost estimating, the evidence is still limited.

Chapter Eight

MATERIALS AND PURCHASED PARTS (MANUFACTURING)

INTRODUCTION

Purchased materials and parts make up a significant portion of the cost of the typical military aircraft, usually about 50 to 70 percent of the cost value stream at the prime level. Organizations that have adopted lean manufacturing attempt to maximize the quality and performance and reduce the costs of purchases, by rationalizing the supply base and carefully partnering with the most important suppliers. Supplier partners help with product design by participating on IPTs and work to support their customers through such techniques as just-in-time delivery to maintain inventory at the lowest possible levels. In this chapter, we describe the characteristics of lean Purchasing and Supplier Management (PSM) in more detail and discuss implementation of lean PSM in the defense aircraft industry, which was for the most part at the early stages. Evidence on particular implementation efforts and findings regarding expected cost savings close the chapter. The full CCDR definition of materials and purchased parts (manufacturing) can be found in Appendix C.

LEAN PSM—A NEW PROCUREMENT STRATEGY

The lean manufacturing model focuses a great deal of attention on efficient operations within the factory, but internal processes are only part of the lean enterprise story. With more than half of the cost stream of a typical aircraft being purchased rather than produced in-house, to implement lean, aircraft manufacturers need to adopt a system of best practice procurement as part of the strategy to reduce cost and improve quality. Every consideration that applies to the value of using lean production within an organization also applies to its use throughout the value chain as a whole. Lean PSM encourages a buyer to look beyond its own boundaries and work with its suppliers to introduce lean production in their production processes as well.

Lean PSM offers two avenues for cost savings. First, proper in-house management of purchasing offers cost saving opportunities through a reduction of people and other in-house resources required to find and certify new suppliers, manage ongoing suppliers, and deal with problems in the supply chain. Second, and with even greater potential for cost reduction and quality improvement, the lean model offers specific guidelines for improved supplier performance based on developing trusting partnerships. Prime contractors and suppliers can work together to improve supplier quality and delivery and reduce costs. Research on best commercial firms shows that the firms have found dramatic savings by focusing attention on suppliers. AMR cut its cost of purchased material by 20 percent over five years (Avery, 1998); Honda of America cut the same costs by 17 percent over four years (Nelson, 1998). Best practice purchasing offers a stark contrast to much of the traditional supplier-prime procurement in aerospace, characterized by more arms-length, short-term relationships with an emphasis on low cost rather than other factors, such as past performance or fewer defects.

What exactly is lean or best practice PSM? Notionally, traditional purchasing views the supplier only as a source of risk, high costs, or quality problems. Tough negotiations are needed to keep the prices down, and relentless inspection is required to ensure part quality. Best practice/lean PSM views suppliers as a source of benefits, as a critical piece of the value chain, as partners in the manufacture of the final product. Trusting, but realistic, relationships and willing supplier implementation of lean obviate much of the need for harsh punitive actions on the part of the prime.

A list of features of traditional and lean PSM demonstrates the contrast and the shift in mindset that lean requires. It should be stated up-front that all aspects of the "traditional" procurement model are not necessarily what has prevailed historically in the defense aircraft industry. In fact, prime contractors have a long history of working with suppliers as the only way to capture the technical expertise held by these other organizations. There has never been a solid wall separating the companies.

Table 8.1 offers a sense of how the lean production system approaches procurement, with a "straw-man" traditional procurement model offered for contrast. Lean's potential benefits are substantial but require restructuring of how goods and services are procured by the purchasing firm.

One first step on the way to gaining the benefits from lean PSM is to reduce the overall number of suppliers and work more closely with

Table 8.1

Summary of Traditional Procurement and Best Practice/Lean Purchasing

Traditional Procurement	Lean Supplier Management
Many suppliers	Fewer suppliers, tiered structure
Outsourcing of individual parts assembled at prime	Outsourcing of components, parts produced at lower tiers, assembled at the first tier
Little concept of value stream	Attention toward the creation of flexible production networks
Arm's-length relationships, no commitment	Closer relationships, long-term commitments
Supplier MilSpec Qualification	Supplier certification
Traditional negotiation, win-lose philosophy	Gainsharing, win-win philosophy
Limited information exchange	Two-way intensive information exchange, emphasis on joint problem-solving, developing new technology
Infrequent deliveries of batch-produced products	JIT production and delivery, synchronized production operations
Inspection of incoming parts	Inspection/qualification of suppliers' processes
Selection based on price	Selection based on best value (performance plus price)
Build-to-print: parts designed at prime, blueprints thrown over wall for supplier to build	Build to performance specification or requirement: early and continuing supplier involvement in design and development
Suppliers not given assistance to resolve problems or improve; substitution of another supplier	Commitment to continuous improvement, working with suppliers to improve their processes

the best ones. Each supplier maintained as a source costs money, including the investment in managing the supplier and keeping the supplier actively on the books. (These in-house supplier management costs are normally captured in the material-handling fee that prime contractors add on to the cost of purchases, which is passed on to the government as part of material costs.)

Although it may seem counterintuitive, cutting the number of suppliers offers a number of avenues for cost reduction. This is counterintuitive because a greater number of suppliers offers more opportunities for competition. However, having many suppliers means that the prime can invest fewer resources in each supplier for helping improve supplier performance, improve quality, and reduce cost. Cutting the number of suppliers allows investments of time and resources to be focused on particular supplier relationships. Firms chosen as partner suppliers are generally given the understanding that the partnership will be ongoing so long as certain requirements of price and performance are met. Suppliers, in turn, invest time and energy to build better and cheaper products faster because they have confidence that they can reap the rewards of those efforts over a longer period. First-tier suppliers in turn can devote resources and management attention to improving the performance of subtier suppliers. The Toyota model includes a check on self-serving behaviors by suppliers; while the car manufacturer may sole-source a component for a particular automobile model (Asanuma, 1985), it maintains at least two sources of that component across all its lines to maintain competition (Richardson, 1993). This may not be possible with the low volumes typical in aerospace, but investing in trusting partnerships with a reduced number of suppliers can keep costs down and performance high.

Two mechanisms can cut suppliers: reducing the number of suppliers offering the same part and moving to a tiered structure. In this case, first-tier top-level suppliers consolidate parts from second-tier suppliers into larger subassemblies.

Note that in best practice PSM, not all suppliers are treated as partners. Given the limits on resources, customers should focus their efforts on suppliers who contribute more to the final product or who would be harder to replace because of their expertise, design, quality, or some other factor. The expense of developing close partnership ties means that potential for improvements—or the uncertainties—have to be significant for this investment to be made. In an example pertinent to aerospace, there may not be a lot of suppliers with the ability to make composite substructures using the resin transfer molding process, so the payoffs of developing a true partnering relationship with that supplier would be more significant than working with a supplier providing, say, rivets and fasteners.

The notional chart division in Figure 8.1 makes some suggestions about strategy.

Suppliers not in the upper right quadrant can still be managed in a lean way. For example, automated procurement, purchase cards, and e-commerce can cut transaction costs with arm's-length sup-

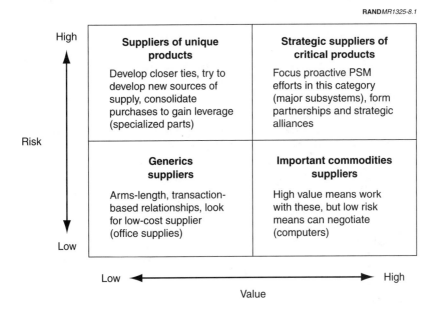

RAND*MR1325-8.1*

	Suppliers of unique products	**Strategic suppliers of critical products**
High	Develop closer ties, try to develop new sources of supply, consolidate purchases to gain leverage (specialized parts)	Focus proactive PSM efforts in this category (major subsystems), form partnerships and strategic alliances
Risk	**Generics suppliers**	**Important commodities suppliers**
Low	Arms-length, transaction-based relationships, look for low-cost supplier (office supplies)	High value means work with these, but low risk means can negotiate (computers)

Low ◄——————————————► High

Value

Figure 8.1—Strategies of Supplier Management[1]

[1]A similar matrix first appeared in Kraljic (1983) and then more recently in Bensaou (1999), Tang (1999), and many others.

pliers. Proactive PSM attempts to migrate suppliers into the partner category, devolving responsibility for design and integration on them as trust increases. Consolidating contracts (i.e., getting partner suppliers to take on the low-volume but high-risk work or the high-volume, low-risk work) is another way to try to get cost and performance improvements from closer ties.

SPECIFIC PRACTICES OF LEAN PSM

A number of specific tools and management techniques have grown up to help firms reduce costs of procured goods and services after the supplier base has eroded. One starting point is the formal analysis of supplier performance to determine who to keep buying from, who to develop a partnering relationship with, who to provide assistance to, and who to stop buying from.

Supplier Qualification and Certification

Lean PSM practices put significant emphasis on quality of purchased parts. As part of this, customer firms generally qualify suppliers as acceptable bidders and certify existing suppliers' processes. For qualification, suppliers have to prove that they meet certain standards, for example, having ISO-9000 approval. (Another benchmark, AS-9000, is providing a core set of standards that should help support lower-cost supplier qualification in the aerospace and defense industry in the same way that QS-9000 has done in the American auto industry.) Certification of suppliers is generally a longer-term process by which suppliers win ratings depending on their performance, quality, and delivery. The best suppliers may have special privileges. Many prime aircraft manufacturers have complex qualification and certification programs that have helped improve supplier quality and delivery over the past few years.

Long-Term Relationships

Part and parcel of developing and maintaining trusting relationships with suppliers is offering them implicit or explicit promises of continued business so long as their performance continues to meet or exceed expectations. Explicit promises may consist of agreements to buy all of a particular item needed during a year or agreements to buy a certain amount in a year or even promises to buy a certain amount over a multiyear period. Often, such promises as these can generate volume discounts from suppliers. The stronger the agreement, the larger the discount. Five percent or so reductions from long-term agreements (LTAs) was one number offered by contractors during data collection.

The term "multiyear contracts" refers to a different kind of promise in defense manufacturing. Because of uncertainties about their own sales, defense contractors often cannot offer firm multiyear contracts to their subcontractors. Because of its general unwillingness to commit to procurements beyond the current budget, Congress will not authorize multiyear agreements unless certain savings targets are met (the exact percentage has varied) or for particular exceptional instances. (Acquisition reform has begun to ease some of these limitations.) Contractual, multiyear purchase commitments by primes to suppliers over a number of years could generate additional savings on top of LTA savings, as suppliers reward their customers for this sales security and for the ability to amortize investments in cost-reduction activities, processes, or manufacturing technology insertion over a larger, stable quantity. Suppliers might not be able to cover the costs of improvements in one year, so they may not be willing or able to make the required investment without firm commitments for multiyear purchases. These are dependent on the ability of the prime contractors to get firm multiyear agreements from DoD and to "flow down" termination liability coverage, at least to key suppliers.

Communications with Suppliers

Lean PSM suggests that formal communication programs that reach out to suppliers offer a number of benefits. For example, newsletters are commonly used to let suppliers know of changes in PSM programs. Supplier councils that meet on a regular basis offer another avenue for communication and provide the opportunity for the customer to get feedback on its practices. The customer can learn if its demands are symptomatic across the supply base or put unique pressures on its suppliers. It is also a way to get some insight into industrywide best practices as suppliers share (nonproprietary) knowledge on practices gained from working with other firms.

Electronic Data Interchange (EDI) with Suppliers

EDI with suppliers is another example of how digital technology has altered industry practices and led to greater efficiencies. The traditional procurement function involved a tremendous volume and time-consuming exchange of paper. Product blueprints, orders, and change orders were sent to suppliers. Suppliers sent paperwork with parts including invoices. Customers sent back paper checks for payment.

Digital technology has allowed the automation of these functions and cut costs dramatically in the process. The term EDI refers to the original systems used to link customers and suppliers. These were often expensive systems that were proprietary to each customer, so that a supplier might need to learn different systems for each customer. Proprietary systems have been replaced by linkages taking place over the Internet, which has reduced the cost and complexity of the linkages. The Internet is also the avenue for other tools that may save money, such as reverse auctions for parts.

Whatever they are called, electronic linkages with suppliers have enabled closer partnering between different organizations. At several sites, for example, suppliers can access the customers' databases to get information on production schedules so that they can plan their own production and delivery schedules accordingly. This was cited by suppliers as important for their ability to efficiently schedule their production of parts and to avoid unexpected rush orders, which disrupted their production lines and increased costs.

Continuous Improvement *Kaizen* Events at Suppliers

Lean practice calls for conscious efforts at continuous improvements in cost and quality. As part of partnering relationships with suppliers, customers often offer considerable assistance to their suppliers to become more efficient. These outreach programs can involve a considerable investment by the customer as engineers and other experts are sent to suppliers for days or weeks for quick or lengthy *kaizen* events. Savings generated by these efforts are ideally shared between the partnering firms so both parties have an interest in making them work.

Examples of aircraft manufacturers holding *kaizen* events at their suppliers are relatively new, although the events that have occurred have resulted in claimed cost savings. It may be that since implementation of lean is relatively new, these firms are focused on leaning their own internal operations first.

Target Costing

The Toyota model of lean production generated an alternative method of setting prices of suppliers. The traditional way is to add up resource inputs and add a profit—the cost-plus model. Suppliers with the lowest bids are chosen to keep costs of the final product down even if their performance is not the best. The Toyota model is market driven. Here, prices are generated by first determining the required target price of the final product based on knowledge of the market. Then the prime will work backward to reduce its own internal costs and establish costs of purchased parts to meet this price. Companies select best performing suppliers and work with them to reduce costs so that their target price can be met. Often, they develop planned-ahead reductions in cost of suppliers' inputs as part of a continuous improvement strategy. Note that DoD's policy of CAIV is something of a move toward the target costing model. CAIV requires trade-offs of requirements in weapons systems in order to meet target prices.

Lean procurement tends to substitute longer-term relationships for competition—it reduces the number of suppliers and deepens the relationship between the buyer and each supplier. A deeper relationship allows the buyer to transfer design and QC responsibilities to each supplier. As these responsibilities transfer, target pricing becomes a useful tool for informing each supplier of what the buyer wants and expects. Target pricing provides a vehicle for an ongoing discussion between buyer and seller about where the costs lie in the provider's process and how they might most effectively be reduced through process adjustments and product redesigns. Target pricing also supports a kind of benchmarking that emulates ongoing competition by forcing a supplier in a long-term relationship to be responsive to changes in the outside market.

Just-in-Time (JIT) Delivery

JIT delivery from suppliers offers many benefits to customers, particularly reduced inventory costs.[2] JIT means that suppliers deliver components to customers exactly when customers need to incorporate those components into the final product. The signal to deliver can be sent electronically, or via an empty container or a message card (*kanban*) sent back to the supplier. Savings to the prime manufacturer come from lower in-house inventory waiting to be worked on, reduced floor space (since the inventory does not need to be stored), reduced labor costs of managing inventory, reduced chance of inventory becoming obsolete and being scrapped, and speedier identification of quality problems at suppliers with faster addressing of problems and lower rework or scrapping costs.

In the lean manufacturing model, JIT delivery requires very close linkages between suppliers and customers so that costs and waste are minimized throughout the production chain. Attention to quality and machine maintenance is critical. In the Toyota automobile manufacturing model, suppliers are located very close to their customers, to minimize travel time between the two factories. Suppliers can make deliveries as often as every hour. When the supplier finishes its components, it immediately kits and ships them to the customer.

However, in actual practice, this is much more difficult to achieve and may have some negative side effects. JIT deliveries have contributed to Japan's heavy traffic (Cusumano, 1994). In the United States, geographic distances between plants tend to be much larger. In the automobile industry, there is some concentration of plants, but aerospace manufacturers have an entirely different set of constraints. They face political pressure when it comes to plant locations, so suppliers of different parts on any particular aircraft may be

---

[2]More information on the costs associated with inventory can be found in the discussions on Direct Manufacturing (Chapter Six) and Overhead, General, and Administrative Costs (Chapter Nine).

located in dozens of states. This presumably increases congressional support and funding for weapons systems but probably is not the least costly way to manufacture products. Transportation costs mean that it may be more cost effective for suppliers to make fewer and larger deliveries. This is economically justifiable given the geographic constraints but means that inventory costs are not reduced as much as they could be.[3] (In any case, the majority of inventory costs lie in work in progress within manufacturing facilities, rather than on the highways in transit. This complication is an example of the different conditions U.S. aerospace manufacturers face, problems they will have to solve themselves rather than by blindly copying the lean auto production model.)

JIT delivery may be required by customers, but unless inventories are reduced throughout the production chain, only a small portion of possible savings can be captured. Ideally, suppliers themselves will only produce their components to order, building a component right before the customer needs it, so that they do not have any finished-goods inventory waiting to be shipped out. (Sending components out immediately reduces costs of holding inventory and also reduces the likelihood of damaged or obsolete goods.) In actual practice, when customers demand JIT delivery, they rarely offer assistance to their suppliers in implementing lean production, so the suppliers must improve their own production processes to be able to manufacture the item right before it is shipped. What often occurs is simply a transfer of inventory locations. Instead of the customer holding inventory on site and using it as needed, the supplier holds the inventory and delivers it only as needed. Generally, companies farther down the supply chain have lower overhead costs so this still saves a small amount, but the cost savings from completely integrating suppliers into pull production are not generated. (These potential savings are the same ones as described in Chapter Six on direct manufacturing.)

---

[3]In aerospace, the issue is even more complex. High volumes in the automobile industry mean that those subcontractors very likely produce parts only for automobile manufacturers and hence would benefit from being close to their customers. Aerospace subcontractors often deliver only a small percentage of their output to aerospace customers, so they would want to be closer to their higher-volume customers instead.

In low-volume long production runs typical in the aerospace industry, two further issues generate deviation from the ideal typical lean production model. Low numbers of final products mean that a supplier may only be producing a few hundred or less of any particular item. It may make most economic sense to produce the entire annual or lifetime quantity of a particular part at once rather than throughout the year or production lifetime. Again, the supplier may end up holding the inventory. Similarly, changes in technology may make some parts of the airplane obsolete in the commercial industry before the production run of the aircraft is complete years later. Unless the prime contractor buys the whole batch up front, it may not be able to buy the part at all later on. Again, economic trade studies can help determine the most efficient way to produce, store, and deliver parts. This way may or may not match that suggested by a lean production model based on a high volume consumer product. Spear and Bowen (1999) provide a reality check to the lean model in their report that, contrary to popular belief, Toyota itself does hold inventory when circumstances require it. However, Toyota also does not consider costs per batch or production lead times as fixed. Consistent effort to cut costs and lead times may help single-piece production go from uneconomic to being the best, most efficient outcome—and this should be the goal.

Examples of JIT delivery were offered at different plants, mostly as a part of small pilot projects. Savings from this particular practice were not quantified. Indeed, as has been discussed, while this may be a lean practice in the high-volume automobile industry, it is not clear to what extent this practice is germane to defense aerospace.

Supplier Management of Inventory at Customer

A related practice seen at several plants was the supplier ownership and management of certain kinds of inventory at the prime contractor. Until the prime contractor actually used the part, integrating it onto the final product, the supplier owned and managed the inventory. This only applied to suppliers of such commodities as fasteners and such equipment wear parts as drill bits. On some production lines, suppliers check fastener bins and refill them as needed. In another example, suppliers stock vending machines with wear parts. Production employees then take parts as needed by flashing their coded ID for inventory control. (This has the side benefit of reducing inventory "shrinkage" from lost or stolen parts.) Information on what has been used is sent automatically to the supplier, who can refill the vending machine when stocks get low.

Supplier Kitting

One lean PSM practice is supplier kitting of parts, instead of the prime contractor putting kits together and giving them to the production workers or not using kits at all. (Refer to Figure 6.3b for an example.) If a supplier sells a group of parts for a particular product, it can package them in kits of parts needed for individual products. For example, a supplier of fasteners can package all the related fasteners required for a particular assembly. Suppliers can also create kits, integrating their parts with kits or parts from other suppliers and then send these integrated kits to the prime contractor. These can be organized by major assembly or product type, so all the parts required for one platform, or for a large assembly, such as a landing gear door, can be in one container. Then further kitting of parts can occur if the prime contractor takes parts and/or kits of parts from different suppliers and consolidates them into one integrated unit.

The greatest potential for savings here is if the subcontractor builds and kits individual parts only at a signal from the prime contractor (rather than to an internal, independent production schedule) and then delivers these kits directly to the prime's factory floor right before they are needed. This reduces the costs of inventory throughout the system. It requires extremely close attention to first-time quality through careful process control throughout the production chain.

SUMMARY RESULTS ON IMPLEMENTATION OF LEAN PSM

We found evidence that all the major aerospace companies had programs intended to reduce their costs through proactive supplier management. Purchased goods and services are typically the largest area of cost concentration within manufacturing firms, so they have been subject to some level of attention everywhere. Levels of implementation did vary, and current efforts tended to be driven by direct cost issues rather than quality or delivery issues. (Prime contractors did report significant and successful efforts in the early 1990s to improve the quality and delivery to schedule performance of their suppliers.)

A common plan was to centralize procurement across different plants of one company and leverage the total amount spent in a particular industrial sector or with a particular contractor. Generally, a large percentage of purchased goods and services comes from a small percentage of the supplier base. Although a few suppliers contribute a high volume and value of goods and services, the majority of suppliers "on the books" sell tiny amounts to their aerospace customers. Managing these suppliers can be expensive, particularly if quality problems develop. These suppliers can be unresponsive to demands of their aerospace customers if aerospace companies are a small percentage of their customer base. Hence, consolidation of contracts across corporate sectors or industry sectors may generate the kind of volumes with any particular supplier to get the attention that the customer wants.

One aircraft prime's final product cost consisted of about 50 percent purchased materials. Three-quarters of the cost of goods purchased was spent at less than 3 percent of the company's suppliers, and inventory made up almost three-quarters of the company's total assets. The company hoped to reduce the supplier base and create partner suppliers, with JIT delivery helping to cut inventory. Also, it hoped to improve the quality of supplier inputs, as rejects and variability were significant costs. It wanted to reduce cycle time by managing lead times of suppliers. Finally, it wanted to reduce the percentage of company personnel staffing the procurement function. The company thought it could save about 4.5 percent on parts with further effort. Savings through 1998 came from outsourcing, personnel efficiencies, group and corporate purchasing agreements, revised contracting methods, and similar efforts. The company saved about three-quarters of its initial target during the summer of 1998 and did better than expected during the final target date of 1999. Future estimates indicate that the company expected to save 1 percent of its total spending in 2000, a figure rising to about 6 percent by 2004.

A second research site was just beginning its implementation of improved supplier management in the summer of 1998 and had no initial savings results to share. The company expected to get savings of 20 percent of total procurement. This number is somewhat more doubtful, particularly since literature on best practice purchasing and supply management generally lists about 5 percent savings as typical, although further savings are not unusual in plants committed to the best practices and working on an ongoing basis with their suppliers. Certainly, 20 percent may be possible in some purchased goods and services categories, but in other categories it may be difficult to get any savings at all. This may be particularly true of commodities with clear market prices, where aerospace makes up only a small percentage of sales.

To summarize, lean supplier management may indeed result in real savings, both directly from reduced cost of materiel and indirectly from such outcomes as higher-quality goods requiring less rework or returns, from JIT inventory with supplier partners, and potentially reduced workload at the prime. Close partnering with suppliers can result in savings as both parties take advantage of the opportunity to learn. Further savings from long-term agreements or multiyear procurements are also possible. Research indicates that savings of about 5 percent are probably achievable in the next several years, provided the manufacturer has a strong, consistent effort to implement the lessons from best practice PSM. Without such commitment, these savings have little chance of being generated.

Chapter Nine

OVERHEAD, GENERAL, AND ADMINISTRATIVE COSTS

INTRODUCTION

Much of the attention to improvements in the factory goes to the most obvious source of cost, the actual production process, which includes manufacturing labor and purchased materials and parts. But direct manufacturing makes up only part of total weapons system cost. Less visible costs in the overhead, general and administrative (G&A) categories are larger than direct labor costs at the prime level, often by a factor of two or more. In this chapter, we discuss how the lean philosophy affects the indirect costs. We present some examples of how companies participating in this study have attempted to cut these costs and the results they achieved. The CCDR definitions for overhead and G&A costs can be found in Appendix C.

THE OVERHEAD AND G&A CCDR CATEGORIES

Overhead and G&A costs provide a catchall for incurred costs that do not fit into the previous cost categories. Overhead costs are those related to fabrication and assembly activities but which cannot realistically be charged on a direct basis to a particular product. Overhead is normally allocated to a base (such as direct labor hours) using a forecast rate (in dollars per hour) called a wrap rate. In general, overhead costs are between 150–250 percent of the cost of a direct labor hour. Factory overhead covers such expenses as electricity, cleaning, heat, plant depreciation, and factory support labor (depending on the company). G&A expenses relate more to the company as an entity and may not be related to activity levels at only one plant, especially in larger aircraft manufacturers. They include such costs as the salaries of the company's front office staff and the like. As a percentage of labor hours, G&A costs tend to be in the 10–25 percent range of the direct factory labor rate.

Far from being an insignificant area of concern, overhead and G&A costs are tremendous drivers of overall weapon system cost. One estimate indicates that overhead costs at the prime are 35 percent of the recurring flyaway costs of the total value stream of costs of the aircraft.[1] However, customers generally have less insight into components of overhead than other areas. Pressure on reducing manufacturing costs has the benefit of having a clear metric—labor hours—as well as an entire cadre of industrial engineers who can offer expert advice on how to make changes to reduce hours, particularly as they relate to manufacturing one aircraft or subsystem. However, overhead and G&A costs do not lend themselves as easily to industrial engineering techniques, and the responsibility for these costs tends to be more diffused within a company. These costs are allocated to all products being designed or manufactured. A key point here is that lean principles must be applied to these costs with equal fervor as they are to the direct manufacturing areas to get real, bottom-line cost reductions at the weapon system level.

ADMINISTRATIVE COSTS

Lean manufacturing includes a number of initiatives that should help minimize administrative costs. One tool is to reduce the number of managers by having decisions made at the "lowest" possible level, that is, by the people closest to the work being done. This also suggests that trained workers have better insight into certain problems than do some senior manager up the chain of command.

Companies that participated in this research did not offer a great deal of insight into any efforts to reduce administrative overhead. They reported a range of between three and six organizational levels separating the lowest- and highest-ranked employees. However, it was impossible to determine if these numbers were really compara-

---

[1]Joint Strike Fighter Program Office estimate.

ble or if plants combined worker and manager categories in different ways.

MATERIALS OVERHEAD

As discussed previously, application of lean to procurement activities should reduce the materials overhead costs at the prime and major subcontractors. Materials overhead (or materials handling costs) has a wide range of values (5–40 percent) of the price to the prime, which vary by company, stage of development (EMD or production), whether special handling is required, volume of the purchased materials, and so forth. No "rule of thumb" savings can be developed for these changes, but application of the lean processes for supplier management should reduce these costs at the prime, major subcontractors, and supplier levels.

ENGINEERING AND MANUFACTURING OVERHEAD

Overhead is a very significant cost driver in both engineering and manufacturing. Indirect labor, employee benefits, the costs of managing the facilities, and the cost of capital equipment are important drivers of total cost and can result in a total per-hour cost per employee that is two or three times the employee's hourly wage rate. As such, it is an area ripe for rationalizing to help reduce final product costs.

Companies did report a number of efforts to help keep costs down, which varied in terms of their being driven by a lean philosophy and the resultant cost savings. Again, many initiatives were presented as being lean that were more accurately attempts to control costs rather than efforts being driven by formal attempts to reduce waste. For example, one firm realized a significant amount of savings by requiring all employees to switch to HMOs for their medical care. Another reported savings of $50,000 per year across the factory by eliminating bottled drinking water dispensers that offered both hot and cold water.

One issue related to the cost of running the factory is an extremely common benchmark of lean manufacturing. This is the issue of factory floor space. Floor space requirements are used as a proxy for lean implementation because the lean model calls for rethinking the way that factories are laid out, a process that quite often results in reduced space requirements. There should also be less space required for inventory storage and so forth. Furthermore, this metric is a relatively unthreatening one for companies to report, as it does not reveal proprietary information, as specific cost data does. In addition, space reduction does not necessarily threaten anyone's job. However, reductions in space requirements only produce real savings in two situations. The first is in a greenfield situation, where a planned production facility can be reduced in size after application of lean principles. (Indeed, one company reported redesigning a planned facility according to lean principles, resulting in a two-thirds reduction in size.) In a brownfield situation, a reduction in space requirements can result in real savings only if another revenue-generating production line can be placed into the freed-up space after lean principles are applied. Savings claimed by freeing up space that is then left unused but still must be environmentally conditioned and kept secure are illusory. Such actions to reduce floor space requirements may reduce the overhead charge to one particular program or product, but if the overall costs remain the same, they are merely reallocated among programs through overhead rate adjustments.

LEAN INVENTORY MANAGEMENT

Inventory consists of three major components, each of which has associated costs. These are purchased materials (parts and materials delivered to the factory and not yet being worked on), WIP inventory, and finished-goods inventory. There are two direct avenues of cost savings from management of inventory: both in the absolute reduction of inventory (increase in inventory turns) and in the way the remaining inventory is managed.

One source of overhead expense that receives tremendous focus in lean manufacturing is the cost of WIP inventory, which is a part of manufacturing overhead. Keeping inventories as low as possible is a critical foundation of lean manufacturing, and that concern drives considerable efforts in all functions across the enterprise. Maintaining a buffer stock of inventory, as is usual in traditional manufacturing, can hide any number of costly problems. Quality problems, machine breakdowns, long setup times, poor housekeeping, problems with suppliers' delivery and quality, problems among the work force, ineffective scheduling, and so forth can be hidden under a stock of inventory. Keeping excess raw material and WIP inventories allows workers to keep working if problems arise in the plant. Machinery breakdowns in one area will not stop production later on in the process if the later process can work on stored WIP.

However, maintaining this buffer of inventory is costly in and of itself and in its attendant problems. Eliminating the buffer forces discovery of solutions to the problems, and hence both cost drivers are reduced. Better management and reduction of inventory requires a major reassessment of processes within the firm. Inventory is such a critical cost driver that it needs to be eliminated throughout the whole production system, including at suppliers. If the costs are anywhere in the system, they will increase the cost of the aircraft. The goal is to reduce the total inventory in the system. The importance of eliminating the buffer of inventory shows up in the very name of lean manufacturing itself—the processes are lean because no buffers are in the system.

In a typical nonlean plant, parts are not being worked on for as much as 99 percent of the time they are on the factory floor. As parts move from one batch-processing cell to another, waiting their turn to be worked on, waste and costs increase. When one company analyzed the flow of a major composite subcomponent through the factory, they found that during 92 percent of the total cycle time, the part was not being worked on, being instead in idle storage or in queue. Transportation amounted to 1 percent of the time, and non-value-added processing consumed 4 percent of the total time. That meant that value-added work was being done to the component only 3 percent of the time that it was on the floor.

RESULTS ON IMPLEMENTATION OF LEAN INVENTORY MANAGEMENT

As part of an overall effort to cut costs, one manufacturing facility began an aggressive approach to inventory management starting in the early 1990s. Many of the specific initiatives related directly to how they work with their suppliers. The company developed a systematic Material Resource Planning (MRP) approach to receiving and holding inventory.

One group of efforts has dramatically smoothed the receiving function. The company invested in technology to read bar codes; currently, about 90 percent of suppliers bar code their shipments. When supplies arrive in the plant, receiving employees use handheld scanners to accept the goods. The scanners use radio frequency technology (receivers are located throughout the plant) to update the inventory on the main computer system. Payment is automatically sent to the suppliers. In 1998, it took less than one day to go from "dock to stock," much faster than the almost five days it had taken five years previously. Supplies are then put in the stock area with small parts being put on shelves. (Ideally, of course, parts would go directly to the production line for installation on an aircraft, but company analysis in this case showed the need for a minimal safety stock of parts.) Each area and shelf has its own bar code, which is also scanned when the part is put there. Locating parts has become a simple task—the inventory computer system can be queried about where items are. This has helped the company achieve an inventory accuracy of more than 99 percent. Cost savings result from lower carrying and storage costs of inventory, less missing inventory, and a decrease in the number of workers required to manage the inventory. Inventory head count as a ratio of manufacturing touch labor decreased from 15 percent in the fourth quarter of 1992, to 12 percent in 1995, to 8 percent in 1998.

The company reported a number of other specific inventory successes. For example, inventories turns increased from four in 1989 to 12 in 1998 and are projected to increase to 20 turns in 2002. Dock-to-stock time fell from 20 days in 1989 to less than one day in 1998 and was projected to fall further to less than half a day in 2002. On-time performance to schedule has risen from 90 percent in 1989 to 99.5 percent in 1998 and is projected to increase to 99.8 percent in 2002.

The results of these improvements are clear from information on the decrease in gross inventory per aircraft equivalent unit from 1994 through 1998. In 1994, the company carried well over $200 million in inventory for every aircraft it built. This figure decreased steadily over the next five-year period, falling to about 50 percent of the original figure.

One measure of savings is based on the carrying cost of inventory. The company did not provide its carrying costs, but generally it is the prime rate plus some percentage. If the assumed rate is 10 percent, savings from inventory reductions between 1994 and 1998 amounted to over $11 million a year per aircraft.

A second plant had not yet engaged in significant efforts to reduce inventory at the time they provided data, but they had embarked upon an initial analysis of the potential savings. In one high-speed machine cell, they calculated that reducing inventory from current levels to an amount that would support *takt*-time production would decrease inventory by more than 80 percent. The eliminated inventory had a value of over $2.5 million. At their stated carrying cost of inventory of 19 percent, the analysis led the company to expect to save almost half a million dollars in carrying costs of inventory per year by reducing inventory in that one cell.

SUMMARY RESULTS OF SAVINGS FROM REDUCED INVENTORY

Firms reported the potential of significant savings from reduced inventory, but actual efforts to reduce inventory have been limited so far. Savings will be from the lower WIP inventory combined with an increase in inventory turns and fewer people needed to manage and maintain the inventory. WIP inventory is expected to be reduced by an average of 50 percent over the long term and about 10 percent with intensive effort in the first year. (This is in line with reports in the literature of inventory reductions from 10 to 50 percent.) Inventory turns should increase by 100 to 350 percent. Direct savings can be calculated by multiplying the amount by which inventory is reduced by the cost of holding the inventory, which is generally the prime rate plus some percentage, combined with fewer people needed to manage the inventory, less floor space needed to store it, and so forth.

FORWARD PRICING RATE AGREEMENTS (FPRAs)

The overhead and G&A areas would seem to provide a way of measuring company success in implementing lean techniques by analyzing overhead and G&A rates over time. These rates, part of the FPRAs at each plant, are negotiated regularly with DoD. Assuming lean is successfully implemented, these rates should decline in real terms over time. Unfortunately, two other factors confound such an analysis. The first is the fluctuating business base at companies. As additional business is added to the overhead and G&A base for calculating rates, the rates will decline. If the company loses business, the rates tend to increase as less activity must support these basically fixed expenses. The other problem in analyzing rates is that companies, because of mergers, acquisitions, divestitures, and other reasons tend to change their accounting practices often, so normalizing rates over time is difficult. Thus, using FPRAs did not prove useful in illustrating that lean implementation was resulting in lowered overhead and G&A costs.

Chapter Ten

MAKING IT WORK—LEAN HUMAN RESOURCES MANAGEMENT

INTRODUCTION

Proper human resources management (HRM) is extremely important in the lean manufacturing system. In a firm that has embraced lean, workers would receive ongoing training to make sure their skills stayed up-to-date. They would have responsibility for checking the quality of their output, and for performing maintenance on their machines to prevent breakdowns. They would participate in *kaizen* events and other continuous improvement activities.

Human resource management is not an independently identified source of cost under the CCDR system. Costs incurred in training direct production workers, for example, are usually reflected in the overhead rates. In fact, aircraft manufacturers offered very limited information on how lean worker management techniques were being implemented in their plants. However, lean manufacturing does offer many insights into workforce issues, and this chapter is included to discuss particular topics in more detail.

LEAN HRM

Literature on lean manufacturing argues that the critical factor in implementing change and tying all the components of the system together is drawing fully on the mental powers of all employees in the production process not just management or engineers. Even the newest mechanics and operators have some insight into the machines, the processes, and the practices based on their day-to-day experiences. This is a source of expertise that can be tapped in any effort to make plants more efficient. As holders of critical expertise, manufacturing operators should be given the authority to make decisions relevant to their work, without having to get approval from a manager for routine decisions. They should also expect to have their suggestions for improvement carefully evaluated for non-routine areas or areas where part and process quality are critically engineered.

Without the assistance and buy-in of all participants in the value chain, organizations will not be able to make the change to lean manufacturing. Womack and Jones (1996, p. 264) suggest that "It has become conventional wisdom that higher levels of management should learn to listen to the primary work team since they know the most about how to get the job done." The authors indicate, however, that this is not quite enough, that workers must be trained to understand pull techniques and in problem-solving methods. In his description of manufacturing improvements at Hughes, Roby (1995) suggests that along with low WIP inventory, early and intensive worker involvement was key.

A number of practices help the workforce contribute to manufacturing improvements. The primary one is management attitude toward production workers—they must be considered resources with the potential to contribute to improvements as well as to actual task completion. The lean HRM philosophy is best summed up by those managers who consider their production workers to also be process engineers.

A second aspect of lean HRM is maintaining a flexible workforce. This has two aspects. First, the workers must receive training on the new methods of production. One lean practice is "operator self-inspection," where production workers are responsible for checking the quality of their output. If they are given this responsibility, they need training on such quality processes as SPC. If they are given responsibility for routine machine maintenance, they must be trained to do this. Both of these skills reduce the need for support personnel on the floor (quality inspectors and maintenance personnel) and reduce machine downtime while workers wait for the support personnel to provide the required services. In addition, the machine operator is in the best position to know when maintenance downtime can be optimally performed, based on forecast machine scheduling. Furthermore, training in root-cause analysis helps workers get to the bottom of production problems and helps reduce their occurrence.

Another method by which lean HRM practice incorporates workers more fully into the production process is by developing production work teams. Workers get a chance to talk about quality and other production issues with others. Teams offer management a formal mechanism to use in tapping their workers' skills and knowledge when trying to solve a production problem or to improve processes through *kaizen* events. As was discussed with reference to product design, IPT structures break down barriers between functions and improve communication. More effective product development and more manufacturable products can result. IPTs can and should operate through the life of the product, not just during the design phase, although their emphasis may change somewhat during each program phase. They should also enable cooperation and communication that can result in fewer levels of management. (The Toyota model calls for self-managed work teams, which were not in evidence anywhere in the defense aircraft sector.)

Matching lean manufacturing's call for flexible machines and work cells is its emphasis on a flexible workforce. With a well-trained workforce and few job classifications, production workers should be able to be reassigned to different processes as needed. Lean HRM practices suggest that workers receive extra pay as they are trained on and become expert on more processes in the plant. Implementing this practice in union plants requires careful management and negotiation, however, as job classification falls into the "wages, hours, and working conditions" negotiation arena. Unions are often loath to give up the accepted and negotiated structure of job classifications because of the fear of attendant loss of power or without other concessions from management. They also seek to avoid a reduction in their membership.

Lean manufacturing calls for a new type of relationship between management and workers, just as it calls for a new type of relationship between the company and its suppliers. Trusting relationships characterized by mutual assistance must replace traditional relationships characterized by insecurity and distrust. This may be more difficult in union plants, but literature suggests that it should be achievable. Trust between management and workers will help alleviate difficulties with simplifying job classifications and may even lead the union to become a helpful force for lean implementation. Literature on the lean model suggests that trust can be built by making a commitment to the workers through employment guarantees. However, making the transition to a leaner and more productive plant means that not as many production workers will be needed. Ideally, lower costs will improve the competitive position of the firm, sales will increase, and layoffs will not be required. This may not be a realistic hope in defense aircraft manufacturing, where volumes are limited. In this industry, one technique is for management to promise employment security for the remaining workforce after an initial round of layoffs. Note that without employment security, getting workers to participate in improving the productivity of the plant could be difficult, because they may try to avoid improving themselves out of a job.

THE DEBATE ON LEAN HRM—EMPOWERMENT OR EXPLOITATION?

Womack et al. (1990) aver that line workers in the lean system are in fact more satisfied with their jobs because of their ability to contribute mentally as well as physically to production. (Workers "think continuously of ways to make the system run smoothly and productively" [p 102].) However, this beneficent view of lean manufacturing as the solution to a century's worth of labor strife is not without its critics. The various essays in Babson's *Lean Work: Empowerment and Exploitation in the Global Auto Industry* (ed., 1995) offer an excellent introduction to the costs and benefits to workers of lean manufacturing. This work suggests that only mixed evidence exists that lean manufacturing benefits workers. In the volume, Parker and Slaughter (1995) argue that lean manufacturing really amounts to "management by stress." Cutting all non-value-added work eliminates buffers that hide production problems and deviations but can mean that workers face continually increasing pressures, without empowerment, as the brief periods that they can allocate as they see fit are removed. MacDuffie (1995) (part of the original IMVP team at MIT) concludes that lean manufacturing offers an enhanced role for production workers, involving "thinking" work, ways to improve production, "team" work, enhanced participation in a social entity, as well as "doing" work. Eaton (1995) compares the exploitation and empowerment approaches and finds that neither is an inevitable outcome under the lean production system. A proactive union approach can help defend workers' well-being. In short, Eaton's perspective is that workers must empower themselves through collective action under lean production just as in mass production.

The overriding message of *Lean Work* is that the idea that the lean production system necessarily leads to fulfilled and empowered factory workers should be reexamined. The lean system may be efficient and produce high profits and competitive advantages. However, managers should not confound their appreciation for cost reduction and quality improvements with worker gratification at making these improvements possible. In fact, Moldaschl and Weber (1998) suggest that the lean manufacturing work organization is merely a modified Taylorist approach.

In their conclusion to a study of an auto factory in Canada, Rinehart, Huxley, and Robertson (1997) agree that rather than being a post-Fordist approach leading to worker harmony, lean production has all too many similarities with mass production, such as a lack of empowerment of workers and all decisions being made by management. Again, this contradicts the arguments of the proponents of lean who state that unless the worker is actually participating in thinking and revising work processes, the plant is not truly lean and implementation of cost savings initiatives will not result in the greatest possible savings. As this argument indicates, the lean manufacturing system does have its critics. Those who claim that lean principles are a means to get increased productivity with or without the willing participation of the workforce may reflect many plants that have incorporated lean concepts like cellular or pull manufacturing. In an industry with excess capacity, such as military aerospace, and a limited number of customers, growing sales as a way of offering job security may be an unrealistic hope.

However, to a certain extent, acceptance of cost reduction initiatives that may result in a reduction of numbers of employees may be inevitable. At plant after plant, the contrast was never between lean or not lean with 100 percent of the workers. Rather, the choice was clear: lean with some percentage of the labor force or not-lean with zero percent of the labor force, as the noncompetitive plant would be forced to close. Under those conditions, issues of exploitation versus empowerment become somewhat moot. In the reality facing the defense aircraft industry, cutting costs and eliminating jobs through lean manufacturing may be the only viable way to survive.

At the same time, the defense aircraft sector faces several near-term ramp-ups in production; for example, as the F/A-18E/F moves to full production, the F-22 joins it, and the JSF starts up in the future. Incorporating insights from lean production means that as production increases, fewer hires should be necessary and costs should be contained.

SUMMARY RESULTS ON IMPLEMENTATION OF LEAN HRM

During data collection, a range of approaches to HRM was visible. It also became clear that some sites have paid more attention to these issues than others. This was evidenced by their response to the questionnaires, with some sites not even bothering to provide answers to these questions. This creates a problem in representing trends or industry averages. Companies not reporting historical headcount or training cannot be truly assessed for lean HRM. Generalizable statements about the industry as a whole cannot be made without this information, as it is likely that the firms with little or no lean-related HRM efforts would be the very same firms that did not respond to these questions.

Companies that did respond indicated that, on average, workers get about 17 hours of training a year. (The low point was 15 hours, and the high point was 24 hours, with four data points.) Percentage of workers participating on teams ranged from 42 percent to 100 percent, with an average of 72 percent. (Nine data points make up this average, with some reports by plant and some by program.) It is impossible at this point to directly link lean human resources practices and lean savings in the defense aircraft sector, both because of limited information on the HRM practices and limited implementation and reporting of savings from lean manufacturing.

The limited evidence regarding the implementation of lean HRM practices indicates that there is a challenge—and an opportunity— for firms who are attempting to improve. The many analysts who suggest that extensive worker involvement is the key to the lean system would be forced to conclude that no defense aircraft manufacturer is entirely lean.

Part III

ISSUES FOR COST ANALYSTS

Chapter Eleven

INTEGRATION AND CHALLENGES
FOR COST ANALYSIS

The preceding description of lean manufacturing and its potential for cost savings provides some insight into the complexity of the system. Further complexities arise when lean manufacturing results (either actual or predicted using pilot programs and initiatives) must be somehow incorporated into formal cost analysis. Some of the challenges cost analysts face are estimating costs and savings when efforts in one particular cost category have results that flow through other cost categories, assessing the effects of lean on historical cost improvement curves, deciding what adjustments are required to incorporate lean into historical CERs, and judging how DoD and the USAF should give credit (i.e., reduce estimated costs) for lean implementation. In this chapter, we discuss these specific issues.

INTEGRATION ACROSS AREAS

Lean manufacturing requires significant shifts in practices throughout the plant, and changes in one particular area may affect costs across different functions. For example, a focus on quality involves up-front design attention to manufacturability; manufacturing processes focused on first-time quality, using such tools as cellular production, visual controls, shadowbox tool storage, and so forth; low inventories to make quality problems immediately obvious; attention to supplier quality processes and willingness to form partnerships with suppliers on quality improvements; and a highly trained, flexible workforce that can perform self inspections. Hence, efforts to improve quality will affect multiple functions in the plant. Lean organizations need to make efforts to tightly couple processes throughout the plant because of these spillovers. Cost-benefit studies of new processes should capture costs and improvements in all areas. However, the very great majority of the lean savings data that plants presented focused on one area (primarily because of the scope of the pilots) with little description of how it would flow to other cost categories. Using traditional cost estimating methodologies, government and industry estimators often assume that lean initiatives that reduce direct manufacturing labor hours will also reduce support hours, overhead, and G&A costs by using fully burdened wrap rates to cost out savings. These assumptions may not reflect actual outcomes when pilots are scaled up across the enterprise, however.

CCDR regulations require companies to collect cost data by lot in particular categories, which broadly are design and development, tooling, quality assurance, direct manufacturing, purchased materials, and overhead and administrative costs. To some extent, this forces attention on costs and benefits of investments in new tools and processes according to these categories. However, as discussed many times in this report, a critical insight of lean is that activities in these different categories can be closely interrelated. Table 11.1 lays out some of the activities that occur in each CCDR category in a lean environment and the interrelationship of each with the others.

It is not the goal of this report to create a checklist of requirements for lean in defense aircraft production, and the preceding table is by no means sufficiently complete to be such a list. Instead, the table can be used by government analysts as a broad tool to address the linkages between the different functions in the organization and to understand how specific lean initiatives may have ripple effects outside their immediate cost category.

LEARNING CURVES, STANDARD HOURS, AND MATERIAL IMPROVEMENT CURVES

A brief, somewhat simplistic review of how a cost estimate is developed for an aircraft will help illuminate the problem facing analysts in how to incorporate lean into their cost estimates.[1]

---

[1] See Lee (1997) for a complete explanation of learning curve theory.

Table 11.1

Exemplar Interrelationships of CCDR Categories

Engineering: Incorporate input from all parties to ensure design is manufacturable, yet meets customer's operational needs and support requirements. Cross-functional teams allow up-front communication of many issues.

- Tooling: When designing tooling, incorporate lean design principles. Minimize set up times. Flexible, reusable, low-cost tooling. Data from design stage can be used as input into CNC machine tools.
- QA: "Design quality in"—pay attention to quality issues in up-front design.
- Manufacturing: Ensure manufacturability up front by considering how parts fit together, unitization, and ergonomics of workers. Ensure DFM/A.
- Purchased materials: Incorporate key suppliers' perspectives in initial design phase to improve design with their expertise and ensure manufacturability of subcomponents up front. Closer link with suppliers to reduce risk of larger, higher-value parts. Easier to manage smaller number of parts in inventory. Fewer suppliers due to fewer parts.
- Support/Overhead Functions: New computer tools change ratio of engineering direct labor to overhead investment in new techniques.

Tooling: Model 3-D solids (CATIA, UNIGRAPHICS). Computers link distantly located engineers, participants on IPTs; up-front concern with part count reduction; fewer tools to design; low inventory requires well-maintained machines.

- QA: Properly designed tooling and tooling concepts can help minimize quality flaws in manufacturing process; attention to ergonomics of tooling reduces damage caused by workers in constricted areas.
- Manufacturing: Flexible tool philosophy; reduction in setup times; HSM allows for unitization, cuts labor cost. Virtual factory models processes to ensure mechanics/machines can physically do work; worker maintenance of tools; computerized work instructions so workers can quickly access instructions.
- Purchased materials: Close relationships with tooling suppliers to minimize costs and maximize tooling technology.
- Support/Overhead Functions: Attention to overhead costs in trade-offs between tooling investment and additional workers; reduced tool inventory reduces overhead costs.

Quality Assurance: Quality data for SPC can be collected, assessed digitally.

- Manufacturing: Emphasis on Six Sigma quality; SPC; 6Ss (housekeeping plus safety). Without inventory, first-time quality becomes more critical as manufacturing cells lose buffers.
- Purchased materials: First-time quality from suppliers reduces need for excess inventory; certification of production processes at suppliers; costs of inspection and returns reduced.
- Support/Overhead Functions: Set up quality monitoring/auditing function; establish training program for worker self-inspection; reduced QA requirement in receiving function.

Table 11.1—continued

Direct Manufacturing: Pull, single-piece manufacturing; flexible, well-trained employees can perform tasks well, also do simple repairs, assess quality problems, make suggestions for improvements; train workers on quality, SPC techniques; work on quality problems, etc.; easier to manufacture items with fewer parts.

- Purchased materials: Suppliers help keep inventory down by delivering parts where needed and only when needed (JIT).
- Support/Overhead Functions: Production rationalized so less space on factory floor needed; attention paid to overhead or reductions in direct labor means fewer direct workers may carry same burden of overhead with increased wrap rates.

Purchased Materials: Best commercial suppliers focus cost reductions and performance improvements. EDI with suppliers—computerized ordering, payment; inventory receiving and management uses bar codes with information sent automatically to manufacturing; automatic payment of suppliers; effective ERP/MRP in place.

- Support/Overhead Functions: Materials handling activities reduced through many initiatives, reducing material burden rate.

Because purchased material, parts, and subassemblies constitute the majority of the value-added costs of an aircraft at the prime, for a production estimate, a list of all purchased materials is compiled (the bill of materials) and prices paid previously for each item (if available) are obtained. After multiplying each of these out for the aircraft, the purchased material is reduced lot by lot in the estimate based on a materials improvement curve. These curves have historical validity as the actual costs of these materials may be reduced by 3–5 percent from the previous lot (probably in part because of learning curves at the subcontractor or supplier level).

Another significant step in the cost estimate is to calculate the required direct labor hours for fabrication and assembly of parts into a completed aircraft. A phenomenon first noted in World War II aircraft production was the reduced hours it took to produce each subsequent lot of aircraft. This phenomenon was termed a learning curve because when cumulative aircraft quantities along with hours per aircraft were plotted on a log-log chart, a very predictable and nearly straight line resulted. With advances in statistical computation packages, these plots can be done arithmetically, resulting in a curved shape on a linear-linear graph. Learning curves varied by phase of manufacture (production, assembly, final assembly, and so forth), type of aircraft, and company but were fairly consistent within each aircraft program. Metal fabrication may have an 85 percent learning curve, while assembly may have a steeper curve of 80 percent, due in part to fewer automated processes used in assembly than in fabrication, so labor hours constitute a higher percentage of total costs in assembly and, hence, lend themselves to "learning."

A wealth of data exists for labor hours expended by lot for historical aircraft production, and these data can be regressed against some physical aspect of the aircraft (weight, for example) to get an hours-per-pound calculation for direct labor hours. These kinds of regressions result in CER models or formulas. An analyst preparing an estimate can access any number of these CERs, enter the physical characteristics of the aircraft, and get the calculated labor hours for the entire production, based on an assumed learning curve. These hours are multiplied by estimated fully burdened labor rates for a particular company by category by year, which converts the hours to dollars. Direct manufacturing labor hours are often multiplied by factors to estimate support functions, such as quality control, recurring tooling hours, and so forth.

Historical learning curves should more correctly be termed cost improvement curves because the successive reduction in labor hours by lot stems from more than workers' learning how to do their tasks more quickly. Industrial engineers develop what are called standard hours for each task or operation that must be performed to produce a finished aircraft. In theory, mechanics could complete their tasks in the number of standard hours if they had all the tools and parts available for their tasks, understood their tasks, had performed them many times before, encountered no difficulties, took no breaks during the day, and were performing value-added work for eight hours per day. As a matter of practical fact, these conditions do not exist in the real world.

Realization factors are developed to predict performance against the standards and are calculated by dividing actual hours required to complete a task by the standard hours. Early in a program, the realization factor may be as high as seven or eight to one, meaning that it is taking seven or eight hours to complete a one hour task. As production continues, realization may approach two to one as a theoretical minimum. Thus, the learning part of the cost improvement curve is described by the realization curve.

But historical cost improvement curves also include reductions in standards, as better tools, equipment, or processes are introduced. One example is when laser projection replaces hard templates in hand layup composite part fabrication. With laser projection, an outline of the required ply location is projected onto the tool, and workers lay down the ply directly without dealing with the hard templates. The work of retrieving the template, placing it on the tool, marking the intended location of the ply, removing the template and returning it to storage disappears. When a new process, such as laser projection, is introduced, a stair step downward on the cost improvement curve would be expected because the new process requires fewer standard hours to complete. This may be partially off-set by a slight loss of realization as the workers learn the new process. In essence, the historical "learning curves" involve literally hundreds of these phenomena over time, as an overall learning curve for the life of the aircraft production line reflects many changes to standards and realization.

With that simplified explanation of the development of a cost esti-mate, the basic question becomes one of deciding whether lean manufacturing should produce savings greater than the historical material improvement curves, whether lean reduces standard hours, realization, or both, and whether reductions observed in historical data were the results of activities similar to lean manufacturing but not termed as such. For example, if under lean standards a more automated process is introduced at the beginning of a program, it would be safe to assume that the hours required to perform the task on the initial aircraft should be lower than previous aircraft produced in the old manual way. This new process should have lower standard hours (at least direct labor hours) than the previous aircraft (called a lower T_1). But the question facing the cost analyst is whether this process would experience the same learning (realization) over time as past programs, because of its lower labor content to begin with, with less human activity (hours) to improve upon. In most auto-mated processes, little reduction occurs in on-machine time after the first few parts are made.

In addition, if lean manufacturing is implemented in the production planning stages, lower T_1s should result as manufacturability prob-lems are eliminated in the design phase, so scrap, rework, and repair should be significantly reduced. With those problems eliminated, can historical cost improvement curves be expected, or should less subsequent improvement (flatter realization) be expected as the normal learning is "shifted forward" on the curve, so that the kind of efficiencies normally experienced on aircraft number 20 may now be achieved on aircraft number 2?

In the purchased material area, are the reductions in supplier prices due to such lean initiatives as strategic sourcing different from the savings traditionally experienced in material improvement curves? Can lean savings be subtracted from these material improvement curve calculations?

Lean manufacturing proponents suggest that because of *kaizen* and continuous improvement philosophies in the lean system, learning curves do not necessarily have to flatten, even in an environment of increasing automation. A sustained focus on sources of waste in the system will lead to continued improvements. However, this contention is by no means universally accepted and in fact was called "the debate of the century" at one manufacturing plant. Using lean manufacturing techniques, they expected a lower first unit cost than predicted using historical CERs but projected ongoing learning curves of from 3 to 7 percent flatter than history would suggest. Other companies offered the counterargument that historical learning can still occur using continuous improvement and other lean tools, a perspective that has also been found in the literature. However, lean implementation in defense aircraft manufacturing is still too sparse and too new to have resulted in conclusive data supporting this argument. Furthermore, much of what companies presented as labor savings from lean manufacturing were really products of increased automation, hence, reductions in standard hours. In these cases, flatter learning curves (realization) should be expected.

But cost analysts in DoD and industry are being badgered to accommodate for claims made by proponents of lean and to reduce their estimates from what traditional CERs and other estimating methodologies would produce. Clearly, if lean practices are successfully implemented throughout all aircraft manufacturing processes, the traditional estimates and methodologies should overestimate costs, all else being equal.

DoD must decide how it will accommodate manufacturers' efforts at improving their processes. There are two main alternatives. The more aggressive approach suggests a wholesale percentage reduction in forecast cost due to lean manufacturing. This entails accepting the prime contractors' claims that they understand lean principles and will be able to transition their pilot project successes to the new aircraft production lines. However, as has been previously described in this report, a number of technological innovations that broadly enhance lean manufacturing and lead to efficiency improvements are already in use on the factory floor and have to some extent been incorporated in the actual hours-per-pound data used in developing cost estimates of aircraft. A global percentage credit would probably involve considerable double counting of recent technological improvements.

The alternative is giving credit to measurable, proven initiatives only. This is a more conservative plan but has some benefits. First, it enforces a standard of measurability on the manufacturers. Specific attention can be given to the avoidance of double counting improvements by requiring that lean improvements be traceable to specific Work Breakdown Structure (WBS) elements and into work and material standards in terms of hours or dollars. However, it may be more complicated, as government personnel will have to examine each initiative individually. Also, it may have the unintended side effect of getting manufacturers to reduce their focus on a major change effort throughout the organization. Rather than a global and integrated transition to lean, this conservative approach focuses on limited improvements. The concern is that companies will respond by focusing their efforts on "low-hanging fruit" rather than on a wholesale alteration of their processes. Larger-scale change efforts may be needed to capture the synergistic efficiencies where proponents of lean manufacturing say the real savings are to be found.

Based on the limited evidence of complete plans among aircraft manufacturers to plot their broad transition to lean, this second conservative approach to estimating lean savings is the one recommended at this time.

In our view, some safe, general assumptions can be made and incorporated into estimating methodologies, although they must be done with extreme care.

- Two separate initiatives designed to reduce labor hours in the production of a particular part should not be calculated against the same baseline. They should be calculated sequentially, so that one reduction should be taken against the baseline and the second reduction be taken against that result (a lower number).

- To the extent that new processes are incorporated into manufacturing, or any other production or support areas, a reduction in the standard hours to perform each task can be applied to the output of historically based CERs as a T_1 (or T_n if applied later) adjustment. These are called displacements from the learning curve. Assuming that loss of learning from the new processes is negligible, this results in a new cost curve parallel to the old one, but with lower values. The question then is whether the new curve should be parallel to the old one, be flatter, or even be steeper. We found insufficient evidence to support any of the three alternatives based on the limited lean implementation data available. An industrial engineer can be very helpful to the cost analyst in determining the adjustments in standard hours, realization, or other factors that could affect the shape of the curve in individual aircraft estimating situations.

- Because the focus of lean is process-oriented in nature, we would expect, however, that traditional learning (realization) will occur at no faster rate than history would suggest (curves should be the same or flatter). Lean may compress more learning in the first units, which may appear to produce steeper curves initially, but these will flatten later.

- Continuous focus on lean will be required to match the slope of historical curves because of the reduction in standard work content earlier (lower T_1s) and compressed learning at the front end with proper lean planning.

- Much of this continuous improvement focus must be highly incentivized, either using "carrots" (perhaps by allowing companies to keep a higher percentage of each dollar they can save) or with "sticks" (hard-nosed negotiating, more dual sourcing with competition incentives). With the government normally negotiating follow-on lot prices using previous lot actual costs (especially in a sole-source environment) and adding profit to that base, contractors must have some incentive to continue the journey to lean and continuously reduce their cost baseline.

- Reductions in material prices may be greater than historical material improvement curves would indicate if primes work with their subcontractors and suppliers in implementing lean. The impact of this approach would have more impact on higher value-added suppliers. Raw material and commercial like purchases should exhibit more of the historical market price phenomena (if there are any reductions at all), especially in areas where DoD buys a small percentage of the overall market. One exception may occur in many large buys of raw materials (group purchasing agreements) where strategic sourcing agreements are used and specific savings may be achievable.

- The overhead area is probably the place with the least likelihood of significant savings. Unless a greenfield facility can be built, aircraft plants must still be illuminated, heated, and protected, whether all the space in a plant is being used or not. Putting more manufacturing into fewer plants and closing others is the only way to reduce costs in the physical plant area. Application of Acquisition Reform (AR) resulting in decreased oversight, fewer unique government requirements, and the use of contractor cost data systems rather than government ones can also help reduce overhead expenses not related to factory operations.

- Support labor, which is often factored from manufacturing labor (QC, for example), may have to be decoupled and estimated on its own. For example, laser ply alignment can reduce fabrication hours for composite parts by 10–15 percent, but the task of inspecting the part does not change, unless inspection technology is improved. Thus, the factor for QC may have to be increased or estimated separately. The same applies to recurring tooling labor. Again, the cost analyst will need the help of a good industrial engineer until historical data that incorporates lean become available.

Many of these techniques have been studied and documented by the aircraft companies. The F-22 Production Cost Reduction Plans (PCRPs) are a compendium of efforts by the tri-companies to reduce the cost of aircraft production. Some of these include lean initiatives. The basic methodology used by both the government and industry estimators was to develop a baseline estimate then apply each PCRP discretely to that baseline to produce their overall estimate of program costs. Until actual costs for the F-22 or other aircraft produced in a lean environment are available, this may be the only viable approach open to cost estimators.

Chapter Twelve

DISCUSSION AND CONCLUSIONS

TRANSITION TO LEAN MANUFACTURING

The components of the lean manufacturing system have been widely publicized over the past few years; how the specific improvement efforts operate to form an efficient synergistic whole is no secret. However, companies that have successfully implemented lean manufacturing throughout their enterprises are the exception. Why have so few firms successfully adopted these techniques? More specifically, why is the lean enterprise model so scarce in defense aircraft production?

One answer lies in the difficulty of enacting any large-scale organizational change, especially one where the benefits to the companies are mixed with costs (as is the case in defense manufacturing, where more efficient production in cost-plus or cost-based contracts means lower profits for the manufacturer). Research on lean manufacturing indicates that it can take up to seven years of consistent effort before the factory is truly lean. And this transition does not just happen but requires a significant commitment and level of effort by the organization, its suppliers, and even its customers. Literature on organizational change recommends a formal, structured approach to change. Successful change efforts require leadership support, a clear vision, a case made for change, communication, training, resources, incentives, and a plan, including pilot projects, full deployment, and, finally, monitoring the change to make sure it is sustained.

Our interviews at airframe contractors showed that it took significant pressure from their customer to spur them to begin implementing lean. In spite of being part of the LAI for five or more years, major contractors pointed to recent DoD or budgetary pressure as the primary reason they instituted pilot programs to test lean principles. Indeed, program office requirements that the contractors "prove out" lean is probably the single most important reason there is any data at all available on lean manufacturing in defense aircraft production. A major airframe subcontractor similarly indicated that customer pressure was the major cause of the focus on cutting costs in their production. One important customer's demand for a 20 percent reduction in costs led the subcontractor to dedicate itself to searching out and eliminating waste within its organization as part of its effort to become more efficient.

It was not clear from the interviews that the prime contractors had a formal approach toward the transition to lean manufacturing. They pointed to pilot projects of varying scales, but RAND's attempts to ascertain what the schedule was for deploying lean principles throughout the plant were not generally successful.

FURTHER DISCUSSION

The pilot projects seen on factory tours combined with a theoretical understanding of how lean works leads us to expect that lean manufacturing has the potential to be a source of savings in military aircraft production. Results from a large number of pilot projects and implementation to a greater or lesser extent at prime contractors indicate that the potential definitely exists. However, the conclusion of this study is that participating aircraft manufacturers have not provided adequate evidence to demonstrate that they are producing in an entirely lean way. This does not mean that they are not trying or will not do so in the future.

Savings estimates from lean manufacturing pilot projects range as high as 66 percent. We would opine more conservatively that savings of between zero and 20 percent against total aircraft historical cost projections based on aircraft built using traditional manufacturing methods are more within the bounds of possibility, assuming that lean is implemented throughout the value chain.[1] Indeed, contrac-

---

[1]The fact that aircraft have become significantly more complex will mean that absolute costs may continue to rise, however. Lean means that DoD can buy more effec-

tors and prime subcontractors in the aircraft industry have already proved out some savings from a number of initiatives and pilot programs and should be given specific credit for the initiatives that have produced real quantifiable cost reductions. Projecting the same across-the-board savings demonstrated in these pilots and initiatives to an entire aircraft is probably being overly generous and may include double counting.

An issue of somewhat more concern is that much of the lean efforts at the aircraft prime manufacturers was focused on reducing the direct labor hours that go into fabrication and assembly. When asked about their lean implementation, the sites visited during the course of this research for the most part described efforts on their factory floors. This signals a very limited view of the lean approach. Some estimates suggest that as little as 10 to 12 percent of the total costs of aircraft production stem from direct manufacturing labor at the prime contractor level. Even a savings of 50 percent of direct labor would result in a savings of only about 5 or 6 percent of total program cost. A more conservative 20 percent savings results in less than a 2.5 percent savings.

For true lean implementation, contractors must focus on the other major cost areas as well, such as purchased materials and overhead. Purchased materials can make up two-thirds of an aircraft cost stream at the prime contractor level. Thus, focusing on generating savings throughout the supply cost stream offers considerably more opportunities for cost reductions. Similarly, a plan for cutting overhead can have significant cost reduction possibilities because overhead may constitute twice the value stream cost as manufacturing labor.

Companies reported many results from lean pilot projects, which generally were in small, localized cells. Direct labor savings results from these pilots were excellent. However, these pilots were rarely on the critical path of the aircraft production process and resulted in direct labor savings that were a minuscule percentage of total product costs. The pilots did not contribute greatly to flow because they

---

tive weapons systems for less than historical models would imply and could conceivably buy aircraft in historical configurations for less than it had in the past.

did not represent areas of bottlenecks in the plant, so overall savings were limited.

It became clear during the course of this research that the greater the size of the effort, the harder it was to get very high savings percentages. Within one work cell, labor hours were reduced by two-thirds. In a major area of the plant, however, savings at this rate would be much more difficult to achieve and would require much more concerted effort. It is impossible to predict potential savings from an entirely lean factory, because no examples of this exist in the military airframe sector. Savings from lean implementation throughout the entire company enterprise were even more remote.

Figure 12.1 graphically summarizes the dilemma about how well the savings results of lean pilots can be used to predict savings at higher levels of a company, incorporating the concern that companies might not implement lean beyond pilot projects.

Figure 12.1 shows three possible savings curves for the ultimate lean manufacturing results. The first (1) and least positive suggests that

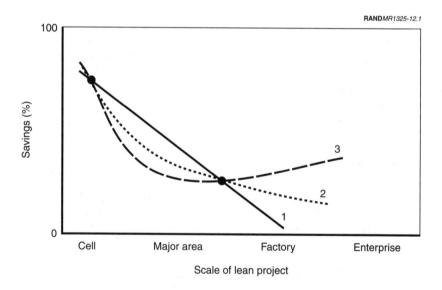

Figure 12.1—Notional Chart: Slope of Savings Curve from Lean Implementation Not Known

companies only implement lean in limited areas throughout the factory, and resulting savings are extremely limited at the plant/enterprise level. The supporting condition for this type of curve is a lack of continued customer pressure for improvements. Without such pressure, the contractor's efforts run into increasing internal resistance with the net effect that no real lean savings occur at more aggregated organizational levels, and the contractor continues with "business as usual" in many areas. In the second case (2), the contractor might try to implement lean savings in the factory, whether through pressure from a particularly powerful customer or a more generalized desire to compete in world markets. In this case, savings are reduced at some higher scope but are nonetheless real and show up in bottom-line aircraft prices. In the third case (3), the contractor makes a genuine commitment to the lean enterprise, not just in the factory, but also across the entire enterprise. Here, exact savings are unpredictable but certainly could grow with the level of management commitment and continued success with larger and larger lean efforts.

The site visits for this project were made in the summer of 1998, and the data reported in this document were collected at that time. In nearly every case, the firms visited reported small successes with their initial lean efforts and had more or less ambitious plans to move forward with implementing lean manufacturing through their factories. One check on how serious the companies are would be to do a second round of data collection to determine if the plants have made further progress in improving their production processes since the 1998 data collection.

In any case, DoD has only one way to guarantee that aircraft contractors keep their costs down. DoD can get better performance out of its contractors if it changes the way it does business. It is not an easy job, although some efforts are being made in this direction. What has to be kept front and center is the fact that lean manufacturing is based on the concept of *continuous improvement in the value stream*. It does not end when the manufacturing line is designed or when the suppliers are chosen. Instead, lean firms engage in a consistent regular attempt to locate sources of waste and reduce associated costs. The pressure to reduce costs never abates.

Hence, by working with its contractors to get them to improve performance continually at all levels of the supply chain, to engage in *kaizen* events to improve manufacturing, and to use the many other lean tools available, DoD should be able to generate improved performance at reasonable prices. In fact, evidence shows that under this approach, the price may even go down (although it remains to be seen if it will decrease more than historically predicted reductions stemming from learning and rate effects). DoD itself is a critical part of instituting lean production at the aircraft manufacturers. It is the final customer and should incorporate the lessons from best practice purchasing and supply management in its dealings with its suppliers of weapons systems. We contend that DoD cannot get out of the PSM game the day it completes source selection. By setting up a system to encourage and monitor improvements in cost and quality, DoD can increase the chances of purchasing future aircraft at reasonable costs.

SUBJECTS OF THREE RAND STUDIES ON INDUSTRY INITIATIVES DESIGNED TO REDUCE THE COST OF PRODUCING MILITARY AIRCRAFT

MR-1370-AF, *Military Airframe Costs: The Effects of Advanced Materials and Manufacturing Processes,* **by Obaid Younossi, Michael Kennedy, and John C. Graser (2001)**

Automated fiber placement

Computer-aided design/computer-aided manufacturing (CAD/CAM)

Electron beam (E-beam) curing

Filament winding

Infrared thermography

High-speed machining

High-performance machining

Hot isostatic press casting

Laser forming of titanium

Laser ply alignment

Laser sherography

Laser ultrasonics

Optical laser ply alignment

Out-of-autoclave curing

Pultrusion

Resin film infusion

Resin transfer molding

Statistical Process Control

Stereolithography

Stitched resin film infusion

Super plastic forming/diffusion bonding

Unitization of aircraft structure

Ultrasonic inspection

Vacuum-assisted resin transfer molding

MR-1329-AF, *An Overview of Acquisition Reform Cost Savings Estimates,* by Mark Lorell and John C. Graser (2001)

Civil-military integration

Commercial-like program structure

Commercial insertion

Commercial off-the-shelf (COTS)

Contractor configuration control

Cost As an Independent Variable (CAIV)

Defense Acquisition Pilot Programs (DAPP)

Federal Acquisition Reform Act (FARA)

Federal Acquisition Streamlining Act (FASA)

Integrated product teams

Military Specifications (Milspecs) reform

"Must cost" targets

Multiyear procurement

Other Transaction Authority (OTA)

Past Performance Value

Procurement Price Commitment Curve

Regulatory and oversight burden reductions

Single process initiative (SPI)

Total System Performance Responsibility (TSPR)

MR-1325-AF, *Military Airframe Acquisition Costs: The Effects of Lean Manufacturing,* by Cynthia Cook and John C. Graser (2001)

Cellular manufacturing

Computer-aided design/computer-aided manufacturing (CAD/CAM)

Continuous flow production

Design for Manufacturing and Assembly (DFM/A)

Electronic Data Interchange (EDI)

Electronic Work Instructions (EWI)

Enterprise Resource Planning (ERP)

First-time quality

Flexible tooling

Integrated Product Teams (IPTs)

Just-in-time (JIT) delivery

Kaizen events

Kitting of parts or tools

Lean Aerospace Initiative (LAI)

Lean enablers

Lean Human Resources Management (HRM)

Lean pilot projects

Operator self-inspection

Production Cost Reduction Plans (PCRPs)

Purchasing and Supplier Management (PSM)

Pull production

Single-piece flow production

Six Sigma quality

Six "Ss" of housekeeping

Statistical Process Control (SPC)

Strategic sourcing agreements

Takt time

Target costing

Three-dimensional (3-D) design systems

Total Productive Maintenance (TPM)

Unitization/part count reduction

Visual manufacturing controls (*Kanban*)

Value (cost) stream analysis

QUESTIONS CONCERNING LEAN IMPLEMENTATION SENT TO MILITARY AIRCRAFT MANUFACTURERS BY RAND

"BEST PRACTICE" MANUFACTURING PRINCIPLES AND PRACTICES

What are the overall **cost implications** of your adoption of any "best practice" or "lean" manufacturing principles and practices? The subsequent questions should help you refine your answers. Please include any important initiatives, practices, or measures that may have been left out. Provide as much **quantifiable data and examples** as possible concerning **savings and costs** of implementation.

Supplier Management

Please tell us in detail about your supplier management programs, including selection, qualification and certification programs, any supplier development programs, strategic alliances, and so forth. In particular, what are the **cost implications** of any or all of the following?

Other specific questions of interest include:

Number of suppliers (in 1998 and 1995)

Percentage of the final product their inputs constitute (in 1998 and 1995)

Purchased materials and parts dollars as a percentage of product costs (in 1998 and 1995)

Operating costs of your company purchasing activities as a percentage of product costs (in 1998 and 1995)

Purchasing employees as a percent of company employees (in 1998 and 1995)

Purchase dollars spent per active supplier (in 1998 and 1995)

Description of what major components your suppliers produce

Shipments received at facilities on time (in 1998 and 1995)

Items rejected by your inspections (in 1998 and 1995)

Percentage of shipments directly to the factory floor (in 1998 and 1995)

Cycle time to award contract from receipt of requirements (in 1998 and 1995)

Description of any "best-value" (rather than "lowest-cost") purchases

Number of and description of long-term agreements. Percentage procured under them.

Number of suppliers with whom you have LTAs (in 1998 and 1995)

Description of Supplier Performance rating systems

Description of Electronic Data Interchange (EDI) with suppliers

Description of formal communications program (e.g., supplier councils, newsletters)

Joint design and development

Description of trends in numbers of suppliers and reduction in competition in sourcing materials and parts that you may have experienced.

Factory Operations

Please tell us in detail about the use of lean systems or other new management techniques in running your factory. In particular, detail recent changes, expenses of these changes, and any cost savings (or cost increases) that resulted. The following list provides some examples of techniques and tools you may have used.

New information systems

Statistical Process Control

ISO 9000/Six Sigma or other quality program

Just-in-time delivery to the production line/ship to shop

New machine tools

Preventative maintenance

Reduction in floor space due to redesigning manufacturing

Reduction in travel time of parts during production

Part-count reduction

Standardization of parts across products

Pull production versus push production

Please provide any metrics you use to measure performance, such as flow efficiency (work time/flow time)

Have you engaged in any pilot projects to test "best practice" or "lean manufacturing" techniques? Please describe.

INVENTORY MANAGEMENT

Describe your inventory system and practices. Have these changed over the last three years? How so? Have you reduced your inventories over the last few years?

What effect do your inventory strategies have on your supplier management or vice versa?

Please supply **cost data about savings** from your current inventory practices versus previous practices.

Please provide any metrics you use to measure performance, such as

Scrap and rework cost, as a percentage of total production costs in 1998.

Cycle time from order to delivery.

Product Design and Development

Please tell us in detail about the use of lean systems or other new management techniques in the design and development process of new products. In particular, detail recent changes, **expenses of these changes, and any cost savings (or cost increases)** that resulted.

Other topics and metrics (beside cost) that we are interested in include:

Co-design with suppliers/collocation

Number of engineering changes

Cycle time.

HUMAN RESOURCES

One of the foundations of "lean manufacturing" is the importance of the labor force in ensuring efficient production. Please provide the following information on your labor force and labor practices.

Number of employees (production, support, and management)

Training hours/employee/year

Output/employee

Number of organizational levels

Percentage of workers on "teams"

How are workers expected to contribute "thinking" work as well as "doing" work to production?

Are workers rewarded for ideas?

Are there any data to support a shift or reduction in costs due to the wider use of IPTs?

CCDR DEFINITIONS

ENGINEERING

The engineering functional category includes the effort and costs expended in the scientific exploration, study, analysis, design, development, evaluation, and redesign of a specific task or work breakdown structure element. Engineering also includes preparation of specifications, drawings, parts, lists, and wiring diagrams; technical coordination between engineering and manufacturing coordination of suppliers; planning for and scheduling of tests; analysis of test results, reduction of data; and preparation of reports. It also includes the determination and specification of requirements for reliability, maintainability, and quality control. Engineering is generally considered to be a basic functional cost category.

Engineering costs may also be subdivided into recurring and nonrecurring components. Nonrecurring engineering costs usually include the costs of all design and development activities through first release of drawings and data. Recurring engineering costs are generally related to sustaining engineering that involves the maintenance and updating of drawings and data and all continuous support of the fabrication, assembly, test, and delivery of contract end items.

TOOLING

The tooling functional category includes equipment and manufacturing aids a contractor acquires, manufacturers, or replaces in the performance of a contract. Examples include jigs, dies, fixtures, molds, patterns, and special gauges. These tools, sometimes called special tools, are of such a specialized nature that their use is limited to the production of supplies or parts or the performance of services particular to the needs of the customer. In military business, the "title" for tooling resides with the customer; in commercial practice, the "title" resides with the contractor.

Tooling costs may also be subdivided into recurring and nonrecurring components. Nonrecurring tooling costs consist of all design and development costs through initial release of basic tooling. Recurring tooling costs are generally related to sustaining tooling that involves the maintenance, repair, modification, and replacement of basic tooling following initial release.

QUALITY CONTROL

The quality control functional category includes activities involving checking, physically inspecting, measuring, and testing the product. Quality control efforts typically focus on manufacturing, shops, receiving and shipping, and records necessary to ensure that hardware, end items, parts, components, processes, and tests are being fabricated, assembled, and tested in accordance with engineering drawings and specifications.

MANUFACTURING

The manufacturing functional category includes the effort and costs expended in the fabrication, assembly, and functional testing of a product or end item. It involves all the processes necessary to convert a raw material into finished items.

Materials and Purchased Parts (Manufacturing)

Materials and purchased parts within the manufacturing functional category include the costs of raw and semifabricated material plus purchased parts used in the manufacture of the specified reporting element. The purchased parts are essentially off-the-shelf items widely used in industry and supplied by a specialized manufacturer who has the proprietary right to the product. The following are examples of materials and purchased parts:

- Raw materials in typically purchased forms and shapes (sheets, bars, rods, etc.).
- Semifabricated materials in typically purchased forms and shapes (wires, cables, fabrics, conduits, tubing, sealing strips, fiberglass, windshield glass, etc.).
- Raw castings and forgings.
- Manufactured proprietary clips, fasteners, hose clamps and assemblies, and seat belts.
- Standard and proprietary valves, cocks, and hydraulic and plumbing fittings and fixtures.
- Standard electrical fittings (conforming to underwriters and other standard specifications).

Purchased parts are distinguished from purchased equipment by cost and complexity.

OVERHEAD

Overhead represents all indirect costs, except G&A expenses, that are properly chargeable for the specified reporting element.

G&A

G&A consists of indirect expenses related to the overall management and administration of the contractor's business unit, including a company's general and executive offices, the cost of such staff services as legal, accounting, public relations, financial and similar expenses, and other general expenses. G&A is also considered a generic term to describe expenses whose beneficial or causal relationship to cost objectives cannot be more accurately assigned to overhead areas for engineering, manufacturing, material, and so on.

BIBLIOGRAPHY

Asanuma, Banri, "The Organization of Parts Purchases in the Japanese Automotive Industry," *Japanese Economic Studies*, Vol. 13, 1985, pp. 32–53.

Avery, Susan, "AMR Lands the Medal!" *Purchasing Magazine*, Vol. 15, September 1998.

Babson, Steve, ed., *Lean Work: Empowerment and Exploitation in the Global Auto Industry*, Detroit, Mich.: Wayne State University Press, 1995.

Bensaou, M., "Portfolios of Buyer-Supplier Relationships," *Sloan Management Review*, Summer 1999.

Berggren, Christian, *Alternatives to Lean Production: Work Organization in the Swedish Auto Industry*, Ithaca, New York: ILR Press, 1992.

Braverman, Harry, *Labor and Monopoly Capital*, New York: Monthly Review Press, 1974.

Cusumano, Michael A., "The Limits of 'Lean,'" *Sloan Management Review*, Summer 1994, pp. 27–32.

Eaton, Adrienne, "The Role of the Union and Employee Involvement in Lean Production," in Steve Babson, ed., *Lean Work: Empowerment and Exploitation in the Global Auto Industry*, Detroit, Mich.: Wayne State University Press, 1995, pp. 70–78.

Gansler, Jacques, remarks to LAI Executive Board Meeting, May 5, 1999, available (to LAI members) at http://lean.mit.edu/private/lai_events/workshops/files/Gansler_Remarks.html.

Goldratt, Eliyahu M., and Jeff Cox, *The Goal,* Croton-on-Hudson, N.Y.: North River Press, 1984.

Imai, Masaaki, *Kaizen: The Key to Japan's Competitive Success,* New York: McGraw-Hill, 1986.

Katzenbach Jon R., and Douglas K. Smith, *The Wisdom of Teams: Creating the High-Performance Organization,* Boston, Mass.: Harvard Business School Press, 1993.

Klier, Thomas H., "Lean Manufacturing: Understanding a New Manufacturing System," *Chicago Fed Letter,* Vol. 67, March 1993, pp. 1–3.

Kotter, John P., *Leading Change,* Boston, Mass: Harvard Business School Press, 1996.

_____, "Leading Change: Why Transformation Efforts Fail," *Harvard Business Review,* March-April 1995.

Kraljic, Peter, "Purchasing Must Become Supply Management," *Harvard Business Review,* September-October 1983.

Lee, David A., *The Cost Analyst's Companion,* McLean, Va.: Logistics Management Institute, 1997.

Leibenstein, Harvey, "Allocative Efficiency vs. 'X-Efficiency,'" *American Economic Review,* Vol. 56, No 3, June 1966, pp. 392–415.

Liker, Jeffrey K., ed., *Becoming Lean: Inside Stories of U.S. Manufacturers,* Portland, Ore.: Productivity Press, 1998.

Liker, Jeffrey K., and Yen-Chun Wu, "Japanese Automakers, U.S. Suppliers, and Supply-Chain Superiority," *Sloan Management Review,* Vol. 42, No. 1, Fall 2000, pp. 81–93.

Lorell, Mark, and John C. Graser, *An Overview of Acquisition Reform Cost Savings Estimates,* Santa Monica, Calif.: RAND, MR-1329-AF, 2001.

MacDuffie, John Paul, "Workers' Roles in Lean Production: The Implications for Worker Representation," in Steve Babson, ed., *Lean Work: Empowerment and Exploitation in the Global Auto Industry*. Detroit, Mich.: Wayne State University Press, 1995, pp. 54–69.

Mayo, Elton, *The Social Problems of an Industrial Civilization*, Boston: Harvard Graduate School of Business, 1945.

Moldaschl, Manfred, and Wolfgang G. Weber, "The 'Three Waves' of Industrial Group Work: Historical Reflections on Current Research on Group Work," *Human Relations*, Vol. 51, No. 3, March 1998, pp. 347–388.

Monden, Yasuhiro, *Toyota Production System*, Norcross, Ga.: Industrial Engineering and Management Press, 1983.

Nelson, David, "Understanding How Strategic Sourcing Differs from Traditional or Tactical Purchasing and How It Can Benefit Your Organization," Institute for International Research Strategic Sourcing Management Conference, February 9–11, 1998.

Office of the Assistant Secretary of Defense (OASD) (Program Analysis and Evaluation), *Contractor Cost Data Reporting Manual*, Contractor Cost Data Reporting Program Office, April 16, 1999.

Office of the Under Secretary of Defense (OUSD/A&T) (Acquisition and Technology), *DoD Guide to Integrated Product and Process Development* (Version 1.0), February 5, 1996, available at http://www.acq.osd.mil/te/pubdocs.html.

_____, memo, "Reengineering the Acquisition Oversight and Review Process," April 28, 1995.

Ohno, Taiichi, *Toyota Production System: Beyond Large-Scale Production*, Portland, Ore.: Productivity Press, 1988. (Originally published in Tokyo, Japan, by Diamond, Inc., in 1978.)

Parker, Mike, and Jane Slaughter, "Unions and Management by Stress," in Steve Babson, ed., *Lean Work: Empowerment and Exploitation in the Global Auto Industry*, Detroit, Mich.: Wayne State University Press, 1995, pp. 41–53.

Richardson, James, "Parallel Sourcing and Supplier Performance in the Japanese Automobile Industry," *Strategic Management Journal*, No. 14, 1993, pp. 339–350.

Rinehart, James, Christopher Huxley, and David Robertson, *Just Another Car Factory? Lean Production and Its Discontents*, Ithaca, N.Y.: ILR Press, 1997.

Roby, Don, "Uncommon Sense: Lean Manufacturing Speeds Cycle Time to Improve Low-Volume Production at Hughes," *National Productivity Review*, Vol. 14, No. 2, Spring 1995, pp. 79–87.

Roethlisberger, F. J., and William J. Dickson, *Management and the Worker*, Cambridge, Mass.: Harvard University Press, 1939.

Schonberger, Richard J., *World Class Manufacturing*, New York: The Free Press, 1986.

Scott, W. Richard, *Organizations: Natural, Rational, and Open Systems*, Upper Saddle River, N.J.: Prentice Hall, 1998 (Fourth ed.).

Sheridan, John H., "Where's the Agility Game Plan?" *Industry Week*, Vol. 245, No. 14, July 15, 1996, pp. 50–52.

Shingo, Shigeo, *A Study of the Toyota Production System from an Industrial Engineering Viewpoint*, Cambridge, Mass.: Productivity Press, 1989. (First translated into English in 1981.)

Smith, Adam, *An Inquiry into the Nature and Causes of the Wealth of Nations*, 1776.

Spear, Steven, and H. Kent Bowen, "Decoding the DNA of the Toyota Production System," *Harvard Business Review*, September-October 1999, pp. 97–106.

Suzaki, Kiyoshi, *The New Manufacturing Challenge: Techniques for Continuous Improvement*, New York: Free Press, 1987.

Tang, Christopher S., "Supplier Relationship Map," *International Journal of Logistics: Research and Applications*, Vol. 2, No. 1, 1999.

Taylor, Frederick W., *The Principles of Scientific Management*, New York: Harper, 1911.

Weinstein, Michael M., "U.S. Industry Back on Its Feet in a Wobbly World," *New York Times*, May 15, 1999, pp. B1, B3.

Womack, James P., and Daniel T. Jones, *Lean Thinking: Banish Waste and Create Wealth in Your Corporation*, New York: Simon & Schuster, 1996.

Womack, James P., Daniel T. Jones, and Daniel Roos, *The Machine that Changed the World*, New York: Rawson Associates, 1990.

Younossi, Obaid, Michael Kennedy, and John C. Graser, *Military Airframe Costs: The Effects of Advanced Materials and Manufacturing Processes*, Santa Monica, Calif.: RAND, MR-1370-AF, 2001.